Minimum Wages, Fringe Benefits, and Working Conditions

Minimum Wages, Fringe Benefits, and Working Conditions

Walter J. Wessels

American Enterprise Institute for Public Policy Research
Washington and London

Walter J. Wessels is assistant professor of economics and business at North Carolina State University.

Library of Congress Cataloging in Publication Data

Wessels, Walter J
    Minimum wages, fringe benefits, and working conditions.

    (AEI studies ; 304)
    1. Wages—Minimum wage—Mathematical models.
2. Non-wage payments—Mathematical models.
3. Hours of labor—Mathematical models. 4. Labor
supply—Mathematical models. I. Title. II. Series: American Enterprise Institute for Public
Policy Research. AEI studies ; 304.
HD4917.W47   331.2'0724   80–25643

ISBN 0–8447–3414–4
ISBN 0–8447–3413–6 (pbk.)

AEI Studies 304

Printed in the United States of America

Contents

List of Tables

List of Figures

Introduction

Minimum wages are widely regarded as having a significant effect on low-wage workers, affecting the value and the stability of their jobs. To improve the formulation and evaluation of public policies affecting low-wage workers, minimum-wage models are needed to identify the benefits and costs of possible changes in the minimum-wage laws. Unfortunately, most of the current minimum-wage models ignore the negative effects that minimum wages can have on the nonwage aspects of work. Instead, most of these models assume that employers do not try to offset their higher mandated wage costs by reducing their nonwage expenditures. As a result, these models have treated the net wage increase due to minimum wages as a measure of its cost to employers. The possibility that these wage increases may in part be offset by employers has been generally ignored.[1]

The assumption that employers do not try to offset their higher mandated wage costs is questionable. It has been a basic assumption of most economists that firms seek to minimize their costs and will thus make offsets. This assumption has proved successful in predicting the actual behavior of firms in many areas. It seems reasonable, then, that this assumption, that firms are cost minimizers, is also applicable to the employers whose wages are increased by a minimum wage. The assumption implies that employers will indeed react to minimum wages by reducing their nonwage expenditures on workers, as well as making any other possible offsets.

---

[1] There are two studies, however, that examine the effects of minimum wages on certain fringe benefits. The first is New York State Department of Labor, Division of Research and Statistics, *Economic Effects of Minimum Wages: The New York Retail Order of 1957–58*, Bulletin B-148 (n.p., 1964). The second is J. Wilson Mixon, *The Minimum Wage and the Job Package*, Bureau of Labor Statistics: Working Paper 32 (Washington, D.C.: U.S. Department of Labor, January 1975). Some of the results of these studies are discussed in chapter 1.

This monograph presents a model of minimum wages that incorporates the assumption that employers react to minimum-wage increases by trying to offset their higher wage costs. These offsets include reducing nonwage expenditures on workers, increasing the effort demanded of workers, and changing the hours of employment. A corollary objective of this monograph is to determine whether the effects predicted by this model do in fact occur.

The main result of this model is that all workers will be made worse off by minimum wages. This result follows from our basic assumption. Employers who are cost minimizers will seek to keep their workers' utility at the level determined by the labor market in which they compete for workers. To do so at the lowest possible cost, they will allocate their expenditures on workers between wages and nonwage benefits so that on the margin an additional dollar spent on money wages yields the same increase in utility as an additional dollar spent on nonwage benefits. Since a minimum wage restrains workers from accepting a lower wage in exchange for more valued nonwage benefits, employers restrained by a minimum wage will offer fewer fringe benefits. Because the dollars then spent on fringe benefits will be more valued than those expended on money wages, an increase in the minimum wage that is offset by an equal reduction in nonwage benefit costs will reduce the utility of workers. This follows because the value of the increased wages is less than the value of the lost nonwage benefits. It is this basic result that generates the prediction that all workers will be harmed by minimum wages.

Another main result is that employers will not be able to offset their mandated increase in wage costs fully, with the consequence that they will reduce the size of their work force. Their disemployed workers will then seek jobs not covered by the minimum wage, lowering wages in those jobs. Thus workers not covered will also be harmed by the minimum wage. It goes without saying that if all workers are made worse off by the minimum wage, there is no theoretical justification for the existence of a minimum wage, at least as judged from the viewpoint of the affected workers.

Chapter 1 describes some of the main offsets employers may make to reduce their minimum-wage costs. Employers may react to a minimum wage by reducing expenditures on fringe benefits, on training workers, and on providing pleasant working conditions. They may make workers work harder and make them come to work during hours of greater convenience for employers than for the workers themselves. They may also lay off workers more readily when business conditions worsen. Each of these offsets has the effect of reducing the utility of workers, thereby offsetting the benefits of higher wages for workers.

Chapter 2 describes the effects of minimum wages when firms do and do not make offsets. By presenting both cases, the predictions of each can be compared with the actual effects of minimum wages, and the better model can then be selected. The chapter also discusses the disemployment and the unemployment effects of minimum wages, since these two effects are different and yet are often confused in the minimum-wage literature.

Chapter 3 also describes the effects of minimum wages under both conditions: when firms do and do not make offsets. It uses graphic and analytic arguments that readers not familiar with economics may find difficult to follow. For these readers, the main results of this chapter are presented in chapter 2, so that chapter 4 may be read next without any loss of continuity.

In these chapters, the minimum-wage model that assumes employers do not make offsets is referred to as the "standard minimum-wage model," since the assumption that firms make no offsets is standard to most of the models in the minimum-wage literature. The model that expands upon the standard model by taking into account the possible negative effects of a minimum-wage increase on non-wage benefits is referred to as the "expanded model." As will become clear, the impact of minimum wages is quite different in these two models.

Chapter 4 examines and tests the predictions of both the expanded and the standard models of minimum wages. It describes the effects of minimum wages on quit rates, rates of labor force participation, and prices. The results suggest that the expanded model is more appropriate for explaining the effects of minimum wages.

1
Offsets to Minimum-Wage Increases

Without a minimum wage restraining wages, employers will supply their workers with nonwage benefits for a good and simple reason: workers are willing to pay for them with lower wages. By observing the job choice decisions of workers in the labor market, employers can discern what wages workers will be willing to accept for jobs offering varying amounts of nonwage benefits. Employers can then offer a certain package of wages and nonwage benefits that will attract and maintain their work force. The nonwage benefits are in turn paid for by the differential between what workers produce and what they are paid. Thus workers can demand more nonwage benefits by being more productive (through expending more effort) or by accepting a lower wage.

At this point it may not seem at all evident that workers will ever accept lower money wages. One need only recall the many violent and massive strikes in this and the past century that resulted when employers sought to lower wages. Still, if we remember that workers are accepting lower wages in exchange for nonwage benefits that they value even more, this acceptance will appear more reasonable. Even on the basis of the most casual of observations, most of us know persons who have accepted lower-paying jobs that offered better nonwage benefits. As an example, consider most professors of economics. On a more substantive level of evidence, L. F. Dunn surveyed low-wage southern textile workers, a group that has been affected in the past by minimum wages and whose experience is thus relevant to our analysis.[1] He asked them how much

---

[1] L. F. Dunn, "Quantifying Nonpecuniary Returns," *Journal of Human Resources*, vol. 12, no. 3 (Summer 1977), pp. 347–59.

they would sacrifice in lower wages or in longer hours of work (at no extra pay) to secure various fringe benefits, including better pensions and an air-conditioned working place. Dunn's results showed that most workers were willing to lower their wages or to increase their work effort to acquire the fringe benefits they desired. As another, and final, piece of evidence, it can be pointed out that almost all firms provide their workers with nonwage benefits, with some firms spending considerable amounts on these benefits. Unless it is argued that these benefits are supplied from a motive of charity, it must be that these firms expect a lower wage than they would otherwise have to pay as an incentive for them to provide these nonwage benefits.

Given that firms supply nonwage benefits to their workers in return for lower wages, the following equation describes how the firm's long-run expenditures on nonwage benefits will be determined:

$$\text{Nonwage expenditures} = \text{Productivity} - \text{Money wages} \quad (1)$$

That is, the differential between (marginal) productivity and the wages of each worker will, in the long run, be used to pay for his nonwage benefits. This equation allows us to categorize the possible responses an employer may make to offset a higher minimum wage:

1. *Reduce money wages.* Although minimum wages restrain hourly wages from being reduced below a certain level, there may be other forms of wages that can be reduced. These include bonus pay and commissions not directly tied to the hours of work. In addition, wage raises can be delayed in anticipation of a minimum-wage increase.

2. *Reduce nonwage expenditures.* Employers can reduce their expenditures on fringe benefits and on the various amenities with which they have been providing workers. From a societal point of view, a particularly important nonwage expenditure that may be reduced finances worker training, a cutback that will affect the future income and productivity of our work force.

3. *Increase productivity.* In the conventional models of minimum wages, the main way firms react to a minimum-wage increase is by raising productivity through cutting back on the work force. Just as, by the law of diminishing returns, more workers reduce the productivity of each worker, fewer workers will raise the productivity of each worker. This offset will not be discussed in this section, since it is incorporated into the demand schedule for labor. Another way to increase each worker's productivity is to require him to apply

5

more effort to his job. Still another way is to change the hours of work to times more convenient and profitable for the firm. This includes not only changing the daily hours of work and the actual time of work but also laying off workers more readily when the demand for output falls, which will result in reduced job stability.

These three types of offsets fully encompass the possibilities implied by equation (1), and they are discussed in turn. Although each is treated separately, I do not wish to imply that employers will not use a combination of all three of these offsets. The objective of this chapter is to point out some of the different ways employers may offset the higher wage costs mandated by a minimum-wage increase. Presenting this wide range of options available to employers will make the possibility that employers do react to a minimum-wage increase by trying to offset its costs seem more likely. Chapter 3 will explain how the level of nonwage expenditures is determined in the first place and how much firms will seek to offset their higher minimum-wage costs. As will be seen in that chapter, they are not usually able to offset those costs fully.

Before exploring the three types of offsets in detail, let us examine some of the offsets employers made in response to an increase in the minimum wage in New York State.

The New York State Minimum Wage

In 1957 New York state passed a minimum-wage order establishing a minimum hourly pay of one dollar for most of the state. The effects of this order on the retail trade, the main industry affected by it, were studied by the New York State Department of Labor's Division of Research and Statistics.[2] Of particular interest, the study investigated in more detail than ever before (or since) how retail stores sought to offset the higher wage costs caused by the minimum-wage order. A mail inquiry was sent to a sample of 9,000 retail stores. Of these, 7,757 replied, constituting 9 percent of the retail establishments and 29 percent of the workers. Responding stores that reported a wage increase at the time of the order were then interviewed to determine what adjustments they had made to offset any higher wage costs they may have had.

Some of the main findings of this survey are reported here; it should be pointed out, however, that they are presented mainly to

---

[2] New York State Department of Labor, Division of Research and Statistics, *Economic Effects of Minimum Wages: The New York Retail Order of 1957–58*, Bulletin B-148 (n.p., 1964).

show some of the forms of offsets firms have made to minimum-wage increases. It is a well-established but often implicit assumption of the social sciences that people neither say what they mean nor mean what they say; the extension of this assumption to the type of survey evidence presented here renders it less useful as any "proof" of the effects of minimum wages. Further, the one-time nature of this survey makes it impossible to rule out the possibility that other factors present at the time of the survey could have caused the observed results.

The offsets that the retail stores made and the number of stores making them are reported in table 1. The second column shows the

TABLE 1

OFFSETS MADE IN RESPONSE TO THE NEW YORK STATE RETAIL TRADE ORDER OF 1957

Type of Offset	Number of Stores Making Offset	Percentage Reporting Factors Other than Wage Order
Wage offsets		
Reduction in ten-hour-day premium	595	5.5
Reduction in daily-guarantee premium	492	13.3
Change in method of wage payment	120	10.5
Nonwage benefit offsets		
Reduction in fringe benefits	136	25.0
Productivity offsets		
Reduction in workers' hours	4,827	20.6
Reduction in employment of extras	1,119	35.1
Reduction in rest and meal periods	192	1.0
Change in work assignment	367	44.7
Other offsets		
Layoffs	690	33.4
Quits not replaced	408	45.0
Price increase	350	95.1
Reduction in store hours	714	22.8
Increase in self-service	220	78.6
All types of offsets	6,758	—

SOURCE: New York State Department of Labor, *Economic Effects of Minimum Wages*.

percentage of stores making the offset that reported factors other than the minimum-wage order as causing them to make it.

Of the 23,220 stores estimated to have minimum-wage costs, 6,758 reported making some form of offset. That is, about 71 percent of the affected stores did not report any offsets. In general, those stores not making any offsets had few affected employees and a small minimum-wage cost (in relation to their total wage payments). Very small stores with one or two employees also tended not to make offsets. Overall, there was a significant positive correlation between minimum-wage costs and offsets. In particular, the savings from the reduction in workers' hours of work, expressed as a percentage of minimum-wage cost, increased as minimum-wage costs increased. This suggests that there may be fixed costs to making offsets such that larger increases in the minimum wage will result in a more than proportional increase in offsets.

The change in the method of payment usually took the form of eliminating commission payments. The reduction in fringe benefits most often was the elimination of year-end bonuses and reduction in paid vacations, sick leave, and holidays. In some instances, profit-sharing agreements were modified and store discount privileges of workers curtailed. The reduction in the employment of extras, as well as the increase in layoffs and quits not replaced, probably increased the work that had to be done by the remaining workers (note that fewer stores reduced their hours). The reduction in rest and meal periods was achieved mainly through the elimination of coffee breaks and by making sure that work began at starting time and ended only at quitting time; once again, this implies more effort on the part of workers. Similarly, changes in work assignments included having clerks handle additional cash registers.

A main form of offset was the reduction in the workers' hours of work. What would have been a minimum-wage cost (per affected worker per week) of $4.82 was reduced to $1.74 for those workers whose hours were reduced. The total potential minimum-wage costs for all stores were reduced by more than 20 percent in this manner. This form of offset could both imply more effort for the remaining workers (given the fewer number of stores reducing their hours) and admit the possibility that stores were cutting back those hours that were least productive (presumably certain hours of the day are likely to generate fewer sales in the retail trade).

From the experience of New York retail establishments with the 1957 minimum-wage order, it is evident that all three forms of offsets described in the introduction were made. These three types of offsets will now be discussed in more detail.

8

Reducing Wage Payments

In the New York survey, stores reacted to the increase in the minimum wage by reducing year-end bonuses, daily-guarantee premiums (paid when the worker does not work a certain minimum number of hours), ten-hour-day premiums, and profit sharing. In addition, firms reduced paid vacations, holidays, and sick leave. These types of wage payments are not affected by a minimum wage and thus constitute an obvious way to offset minimum-wage costs.

A form of wage reduction that has not been considered in the minimum-wage literature but may be important for interpreting the impact of minimum-wage increases is the reduction of wages before a minimum-wage increase. This form of offset is available when firms can anticipate the timing and size of future increases in the minimum wage. To illustrate, assume that, in the absence of a minimum wage, a worker produces and earns $1.00 an hour for the first two years he is in a job and produces and earns $2.00 an hour subsequently. Now suppose that a new minimum wage of $1.50 an hour is passed and will be imposed at the beginning of the second year. An employer can offset the minimum wage by paying the worker only $0.50 in his first year, $1.50 in his second year, and $2.00 after that. (Note that we are ignoring, for expository reasons, the effect of interest rates here.) The worker will not quit his job, since its present value is the same as in the absence of the minimum wage. Any firm paying $1.00 in the first year will be at a competitive disadvantage in terms of goods sold with respect to the firms paying $0.50. Thus it is possible in this case for an employer to offset the effects of a minimum-wage increase if he can anticipate when it will go into effect. Table 2 shows the history of past minimum-wage increases and indicates how far ahead each could have been anticipated. The table shows when the Fair Labor Standards Act was amended to raise the minimum wage, the wages that were approved, and the effective date of each wage.

To some degree, employers would have been able to anticipate the passage of new minimum-wage levels from the debate that preceded them. Since the subsequent increases in the minimum wage, incorporated in the amendments, could be anticipated with even more certainty, they should have had, according to this analysis, a smaller relative impact than the initial increases legislated in each amendment. This conjecture is tested in chapter 4.

Another, similar form of wage offset is to delay a wage raise that would otherise have occurred after a minimum-wage increase. To illustrate, assume that in the case described the employer was

9

TABLE 2

DATES OF MINIMUM-WAGE AMENDMENTS

Date of Amendment	Minimum-Wage Rate ($)[a]	Effective Date of Wage[b]
June 1938	0.25	October 1938
	0.30	October 1939
October 1949	0.75	January 22, 1950
August 1955	1.00	March 1956
May 1961	1.15	September 1961
	1.25	September 1963
September 1966	1.40	February 1967
	1.60	February 1968
March 1974	2.00	May 1974
	2.10	January 1975
	2.30	January 1976
October 1977	2.65	January 1978
	2.90	January 1979
	3.10	January 1980
	3.35	January 1981

[a] The minimum wages and dates for newly covered workers are not reported.
[b] Unless stated otherwise, the effective date is at the first of the month.

surprised by the minimum wage of $1.50 at the beginning of the second year. He could offset this cost if he could pay his worker $1.50 in his third year (instead of the $2.00 the worker would otherwise have earned). This possibility is severely limited, however, by the competition of other employers for the worker. Since this worker will presumably also produce $2.00 an hour for them, the other employers will be willing to bid his hourly wage up to $2.00. The employer may be able to offset some of the minimum-wage cost by paying a wage lower than $2.00 in the third year if the worker's costs of searching for and finding a better-paying job are substantial. The greater the worker's search costs, the more the employer can delay increasing the worker's wage, but clearly this offset is not likely to be as great as the offset possible when the minimum-wage increase can be anticipated.

Reducing Nonwage Expenditures

A substantial proportion of the average worker's costs to his employer are in the form of fringe benefits and paid leave. In 1971, 21 percent of the payroll of all companies was spent on voluntary fringe benefits and paid leave. This percentage does not include the expenditures firms make to provide safe, clean, and attractive working environments, nor does it include the costs of providing a more humane form of management (for example, the costs of communicating with workers and providing them with a grievance procedure). For lower-wage workers (those who will be most affected by a minimum-wage increase), however, this percentage is substantially smaller. For example, in 1972 (when the minimum wage was $1.60, where it remained until its increase to $2.00 in 1974), workers earning $2.00 or less received the benefits shown in table 3.

The sum of the benefits in table 3 represented 1.84 percent of the payroll of firms paying $2.00 or less on the average. Because of the small amount, the possible reduction of these expenditures represents only a small offset against most minimum-wage increases.

Nevertheless, employers make many other forms of expenditures for their workers that are rarely accounted for because they are difficult to measure, for example, funds spent for more pleasant working conditions. Let us consider an example of poor working conditions. An article in the *Wall Street Journal* (March 19, 1979) titled "Low Pay, Bossy Bosses Kill Kids' Enthusiasm for Food-Service Jobs" detailed how food-service workers must put up with poor working conditions and autocratic bosses. Many managers are reported to be twenty-year-olds without any training in employee relations. As one worker reported, the managers "are real snotty. They yell at the workers in front of customers and call you stupid." Since the article notes that many of these jobs are paying the minimum wage, such

---

TABLE 3

BENEFITS OF NONOFFICE EMPLOYEES IN ESTABLISHMENTS PAYING TWO
DOLLARS OR LESS IN AVERAGE HOURLY COMPENSATION

Benefit	Percentage of Workers Receiving Benefit	Expenditures as Percentage of Payroll of Firms Having Benefit
Paid leave (except sick leave)	58	2.2
Private retirement plan	3	1.8
Private life, accident, and health insurance	27	1.9

SOURCE: U.S. Department of Labor, Bureau of Labor Statistics, *Employee Compensation in the Private Non-farm Economy, 1972*, Bureau of Labor Statistics Bulletin 1875 (Washington, D.C.: U.S. Government Printing Office, 1975), tables 23, 24, 25.

working conditions may reflect the employers' reduction in expenditures for better and more courteous managers. The article also notes that the turnover rate of fast-food employers is very high, equaling 300 percent annually. The high turnover rate may in part be explained by the prediction of the expanded model that minimum wages will lower rather than raise the value of the jobs they affect.

One form of nonwage expenditures relevant to the job horizons of many young workers involves on-the-job training. Even those jobs not having formal training programs may have as costs the mistakes and lower productivity of new workers. The experience and training that young workers acquire on their first jobs are important to their future earnings, but with a minimum wage preventing firms from passing the costs of training to new workers in the form of lower wages, employers may instead seek older, more experienced workers. Welch, for example, found that the employment of teenagers had dropped relatively more in those industries covered by the minimum wage.[3] He notes: "In 1930, manufacturing was by far the largest teenage employer, accounting for roughly 40 percent of all jobs. . . . By 1955 the teenage share of all manufacturing jobs had fallen to half the earlier level."[4] As another example, he notes that the proportion of teenagers employed in retail establishments fell after the minimum-wage coverage had been extended to that industry. In summary, he states that with the increasing coverage of the minimum-wage law, "there are fewer and fewer uncovered jobs for teenagers to turn to for employment."[5]

Increasing Productivity

When economists describe the demand-for-labor schedule, they are describing the effects of a higher cost per worker on the employer's choice of his work force size and of his method of producing output. In general, a higher cost per worker causes employers to hire fewer workers and to use methods of producing output that require fewer workers per unit of output. Both of these adjustments raise the productivity per worker and allow the employer to meet his higher cost per worker.[6] When the minimum wage is increased, two ad-

---

[3] Finis Welch, *Minimum Wages* (Washington, D.C.: American Enterprise Institute, 1978).
[4] Welch, *Minimum Wages*, pp. 31–32. Note that the minimum wage was passed in 1938.
[5] Welch, *Minimum Wages*, p. 32.
[6] The "shock theory" of minimum wages (which holds that minimum wages shock firms into being more efficient) can be introduced into the demand curve for labor. That less labor will probably be demanded at higher wages, even in the presence of the shock theory, is argued in chapter 2.

ditional methods of raising a worker's productivity can be employed: increasing the effort demanded of each worker and changing the hours of work to those more convenient for the employer. The reason these adjustments are not generally considered in constructing the demand-for-labor schedule is that increased cost per worker is assumed to be derived from a marketwide increase in the demand for labor.[7] In this case, if employers ask more effort of their workers or give them more inconvenient hours to work, the workers will quit and take a job from another employer unless their wages are increased even more than pay industrywide. In the case of a minimum-wage increase, however, the demand for labor has not been increased; instead, fewer jobs are available to quitting workers. Thus employers can, without any wage cost beyond that of the minimum wage, demand more effort from their workers and alter their hours. We will now discuss these two forms of offsets in more detail.

A worker sells to an employer not only his time but also what is often referred to as his effort. "Effort" refers to many dimensions, including the physical, the mental, and the psychological. The classic illustration of these dimensions is the form of protest known as "working by the book": production quickly comes to a halt when workers do only what they are told to do. Just as work time reduces a worker's leisure, so work effort diminishes his ability to enjoy his leisure. An increase in the minimum wage allows an employer to demand more effort from his workers, which thereby reduces the value of the job to his workers. As an example of a form that demanding more effort may take, an employer can assign the tasks of disemployed workers to his current workers, thereby increasing the effort they must expend and reducing the net cost of a minimum-wage increase.

Another way to increase the productivity per worker is to change the hours of work. This possibility is open to only some employers, and we will now discuss two of the main cases.

For many employers, the value of what a worker produces depends on when he produces it. For example, a worker's productivity will vary from hour to hour in a retail store or a restaurant as there are more or fewer customers at different times of the day. Certain products are worth more during certain seasons of the year; the services of an ice cream salesman or a lifeguard, for example, will have higher value in the summer months than during the rest of the year. Over the business cycle, output produced during periods of peak demand is more highly valued than that produced during

---

[7] Alternatively, the increase in wages may be imposed by a union, which will also bargain for and seek to maintain the positive nonwage aspects of work.

periods of weak demand, especially when inventory costs are high. In all these cases, if employers had no turnover costs and workers incurred no cost in going to and from work, employers could instantaneously adjust their labor force so that their workers had the same marginal productivity in all periods. In fact, though, the labor market is not frictionless—both employers and workers have considerable adjustment costs for beginning and ending work. Because of these frictions, employers will have workers at some times producing more than the employer is spending on them and at other times producing less.

For these employers, a minimum-wage increase will cause them to reduce their workers' hours of work by cutting back on the less productive hours. This in turn allows the average productivity of each worker to increase and covers at least some of the costs of the minimum wage. Correspondingly, the workers' welfare will be reduced since they do not want fewer hours of work.

This form of offset will often take the form of fewer hours of work per day or per week. The survey of New York retail employers reported that one of the main forms of offsets was to reduce the workers' hours on the job. For employers who took this course of action, more than 64 percent of the potential minimum-wage cost was offset by fewer hours of work. There is also some evidence that many employers economywide make this form of offset. For example, Zucker found that past minimum-wage increases have resulted in a greater reduction in man-hours than in workers, implying that employers have reduced the hours of work per worker.[8] Similarly, Gramlich found that more full-time workers than part-time workers were disemployed by past minimum-wage increases.[9]

Another form in which this type of offset may occur is on a cyclical basis as reduced job stability and shorter job tenure for minimum-wage workers. A study by Koster and Welch indicates that the minimum-wage law has rendered low-wage workers (and in particular teen-agers) more vulnerable to the vicissitudes of the business cycle.[10] To describe this form of offset in somewhat newer terminology, the minimum-wage law has caused the workers whose

---

[8] Albert Zucker, "Minimum Wages and the Long-Run Elasticity of Demand for Labor," *Quarterly Journal of Economics*, vol. 87 (May 1973), pp. 267–77.
[9] Edward M. Gramlich, *Impact of Minimum Wages on Other Wages, Employment, and Family Income*, Brooking Papers on Economic Activity no. 2 (Washington, D.C.: Brookings Institution, 1976), pp. 409–51.
[10] Marvin Kosters and Finis Welch, "The Effects of Minimum Wages on the Distribution of Changes in Aggregate Employment," *American Economic Review*, vol. 62, no. 3 (June 1972), pp. 323–32.

wages it affects to become the last to be hired and the first to be fired.

In contrast, other employers may offset part of the costs of the minimum wage by increasing their hours of work. This possibility occurs when the firm has a daily fixed cost for engaging a worker to do a job.[11] To cover this cost, the worker must produce, during each hour of his work, more than the firm is spending on him during each hour. The resulting hourly differential between productivity and pay, when multiplied by the daily hours of work, will cover the daily fixed cost of engaging the worker. An increase in the minimum wage may cause these firms to increase their hours of work. Mixon found that several low-wage industries reacted to a minimum-wage increase in this manner, increasing both their regular hours of work and their overtime hours.[12]

As can be seen from both of the cases described, it is not certain whether an increase in the minimum wage will lead to an increase or a decrease in the daily hours of work. It appears more likely, though, that the minimum wage has led to shorter job tenure and greater turnover in the jobs it affects. It would also seem from the theory described that an increase in the variance of the working hours for differing jobs, as well as a reduction in the proportion of jobs having the convenient daily hours of work desired by workers, will result from a minimum-wage increase. These effects will not only reduce the utility of the workers in these jobs but will also make the search for acceptable jobs more difficult for the unemployed.

Summary

Some of the offsets that employers may attempt to make in reaction to an increase in the minimum wage have been described in detail in this chapter. Employers may reduce those wage payments not tied directly to the hours of work; they may reduce nonwage expenditures; they may demand more effort from their workers; and they may alter their hours of work. These ways are by no means exhaustive; employers in the quest for more profits have a greater incentive than I do to find means to reduce their costs. The main point of this chapter is simply that employers do have many options

[11] Of course, the fixed cost could also be a weekly fixed cost, and the hours of work, the weekly hours of work. For longer periods of time, the employer paying a straight hourly wage may have difficulty ensuring that workers will work extra hours, so that this analysis applies mainly to shorter periods.

[12] J. Wilson Mixon, *The Minimum Wage and the Job Package*, Bureau of Labor Statistics Working Paper 32 (Washington, D.C.: U.S. Department of Labor, January 1975).

available to them to offset at least some of the costs of a minimum-wage increase. It therefore seems likely, at least when the increase substantially affects their costs, that they will exercise some of these options. If they do, it will be necessary for us to model the effects of minimum wages by taking into account the effects of these offsets.

2

The Effects of Minimum Wages
on the Labor Force

Chapter 1 examined some of the offsets employers may make in reaction to a minimum-wage increase. This chapter examines the effects of minimum wages when employers do and do not make offsets. The effects of minimum wages when employers do not make offsets will be described by what I will call the standard model of minimum wages,[1] and the effects when employers do make offsets will be referred to as the expanded model. Although expanding the standard model by assuming that firms do make offsets may seem minor, in fact the predicted consequences of a minimum-wage increase are quite different. In particular, in the expanded model, workers whose wages are increased by the minimum wage are in net terms made worse off because of the offsets made by their employers.

This chapter outlines the basic assumptions of both the standard and the expanded models of minimum wages and presents their predictions. Chapter 3 presents these models in more detail, and chapter 4 compares their predictions. Why present the standard model at all if it is, as I believe, wrong? There are several reasons. First, using the standard model with the expanded model will make it possible to differentiate the predictions of both and to determine which is more appropriate for describing the effects of minimum wages. Determining the relevance of these models is important, since their welfare implications differ so radically. A second reason for presenting the standard model is that many of its features are common to the expanded model; by presenting such features here, it will be clearer to the reader that they are not the essential aspects

---

[1] The main development of the standard model of minimum wages is in Jacob Mincer, "Unemployment Effects of Minimum Wages," *Journal of Political Economy*, vol. 84, no. 4, pt. 2 (August 1976), supplement, pp. 87–104.

that cause the difference in results between the two models. A final reason is that where employers can make no further offsets (or, for some reason, choose not to make any further offsets), the standard model's results will apply. Thus the effects of a minimum-wage increase may in part be explained by the expanded model (to the point where employers stop making offsets), with the remaining part being explained by the standard model.

A Confusion

In a recent survey, economists were asked whether they agreed with the proposition, "A minimum wage increases unemployment among young and unskilled workers."[2] More than 68 percent of the responding economists generally agreed with this proposition, and only 10 percent disagreed. In fact, of the thirty questions asked, this proposition had one of the highest levels of approval. Unfortunately, there is no theoretical reason for it to be true, and there is at best only weak support for it empirically. The main point of presenting this question, then, is that it reflects a major confusion in the economic literature on the minimum wage: the confounding of the meanings of unemployment and disemployment. A minimum wage will result in a reduction in the work force of those firms affected by it, causing more workers to become disemployed. Depending upon what the disemployed do, however, the number of unemployed workers searching for work may increase or decrease. As we shall see in this chapter, a minimum-wage increase can either increase or decrease unemployment, although it always causes disemployment.

A variation of this confusion comes in the way changes in unemployment caused by a minimum-wage increase are interpreted. For years the proponents of minimum wages have claimed that minimum wages do not increase unemployment. What they do not seem to understand is that if unemployment is truly not affected, then by implication the minimum wage has made a substantial proportion of the work force worse off. (This result is discussed later.) As a consequence of the confusion between disemployment and unemployment, we have the odd spectacle of advocates for the minimum wage using evidence suggesting that minimum wages are harmful.

To unravel the confusion between unemployment and disem-

---

[2] J. R. Kearl, Clayne L. Pope, Gordon C. Whiting, and Larry T. Wimmer, "A Confusion of Economists?" *American Economic Review*, vol. 69, no. 2 (May 1979), pp. 28–37.

ployment, let us look at a model of minimum wages developed by Jacob Mincer.[3] To present this model, we shall examine how the various components of the labor force, including unemployment, labor force participation, and employment, are determined.

What Does Unemployment Mean?

An unemployed worker is one who is searching for a new job or who is waiting to be recalled to his last job. Unemployment, however, occurs in many parts of our economy. In most areas, for example, there are usually a few restaurants that always seem to have a line of patrons waiting for a table. These patrons are in a sense "unemployed," in that they are waiting to eat but are not currently eating. Continuing with this example, what can be said about the quality of a restaurant from the length of its "unemployment line"? On the positive side, the restaurant may be truly superior, so that it can draw a crowd that exceeds its capacity. On the negative side, however, it may have a large crowd only because the other restaurants in the area are horrible or there are too few restaurants in the area. In sum, then, we cannot tell from the unemployment lines at restaurants how good the restaurants are or how good dining conditions in the area are.

Just as we cannot evaluate the quality of a restaurant by the length of its waiting line, we cannot tell just from the rate of unemployment in the work force how well workers are doing. Higher unemployment (following, for example, a minimum-wage increase) could be the result either of a better or of a poorer labor market. In a better labor market, it might mean that more superior jobs are becoming available, so that more workers become unemployed to seek those better jobs, just as better restaurants in the example above might have longer waiting lines. In poorer labor markets, on the other hand, higher unemployment might mean that there are few acceptable jobs, just as a restaurant in an area with few restaurants may have longer lines of waiting customers. Thus higher unemployment can occur in both better and poorer labor markets. Generally, over the business cycle, the second case dominates, so that unemployment increases when employment falls.

The same need not be true of minimum wages, however: lower unemployment need not signify better working conditions, nor does higher unemployment necessarily imply that workers are worse off.

---

[3] Mincer, "Unemployment Effects of Minimum Wages."

19

To illustrate, assume that a minimum wage raises the value of all minimum-wage jobs but does not affect either employment or the availability of jobs. Obviously, more workers will become unemployed to seek the better minimum-wage jobs, and this increase in unemployment will reflect an improvement, not a deterioration, in the welfare of workers. To understand the welfare effects of minimum wages better, we will now analyze the main components of the labor force and how they are determined.

Labor Force Participation

The size of the labor force equals the number of persons who feel they are better off working or actively seeking work. Potential entrants to the labor force compare their value of participating in the labor force by seeking work (which we will call their search income) with their value of not working (which we will call nonwork income).[4] Those who find their search income exceeding their nonwork income will enter the labor force. It follows, then, that an increase in search income will, other things being the same, increase the size of the labor force.

An increase in the minimum wage will mainly affect the size of the labor force through its effects on search income, which it affects in two ways. First, a minimum-wage increase changes the value of jobs: in the standard model, it increases the value of jobs; in the expanded model, it decreases it (as we will show below). Second, in both models the increase reduces the number of job openings, making the search for work both more difficult and more costly. In the standard model, the net impact of minimum wages on search income is uncertain: the increased value of jobs raises search income, but the increased difficulty of finding work reduces search income. In the expanded model, both the effects of minimum wages act to reduce search income (and, as a consequence, the size of the labor force).

Employment

The number of workers that employers will hire is a negative function of the employers' cost per worker. In terms of the standard model, where fringe benefits and other nonwage costs are ignored, the level of employment is a negative function of the wage rate: at higher wage rates, fewer workers will be employed. This well-known re-

---

[4] More precisely, nonwork income is defined as the smallest hypothetical income necessary to cause an individual to enter the labor force for even a few hours of work.

lationship will not be discussed here except to comment on two objections sometimes raised to it. First, it is sometimes argued that the higher wage costs of a minimum wage will be offset by a higher demand for output generated by the workers who are now better paid, so that employment will not fall. This argument could be valid only in a closed economy and then only under certain conditions, but it is not valid in an open economy. Since only a small number of workers are affected by a minimum wage, effects of that wage must be described with an open economy model, where a higher wage will lead to less employment.

A second objection comes from the shock model,[5] which holds that a minimum-wage increase shocks previously inefficient employers into using their labor more efficiently, possibly even lowering costs and prices and thereby allowing more output to be sold, with a possible net zero effect on employment. Note that for this result to occur, it must be true that employers are very inept, since they are assumed by the shock model not to exploit even those efficiencies that will lead to a significantly larger profit. If a minimum wage is not to reduce employment, these efficiencies must be so large, given the size of past minimum-wage increases, that they are capable of increasing the profits of firms 50 percent or more.[6] It is difficult to believe that such opportunities are consistently overlooked by the majority of employers in the competitive markets that most low-wage employers operate in. Note also that any efficiency an employer adopts is likely to be labor-saving, so that even if output is not reduced, disemployment will still occur.[7] Only under rather stringent

[5] The shock model is described in John M. Peterson and Charles T. Stewart, Jr., *Employment Effects of Minimum Wage Rates* (Washington, D.C.: American Enterprise Institute, 1969), p. 29.

[6] Consider a somewhat typical firm whose labor costs represent 60 percent of its total sales and whose profits are 10 percent of total sales, capital costs accounting for the remaining 30 percent. If a minimum-wage increase of 10 percent can be offset by greater efficiencies, this firm could have achieved a 60 percent increase in profits (to 16 percent of total sales), since the minimum-wage increase would otherwise have raised total labor costs to about 66 percent of total costs. The larger the share of labor and the smaller the share of profits, the greater the potential increase in profits and the more unreasonable is the shock theory's assumption that employers will ignore such large efficiencies.

[7] A discussion of the shock theory and its implied effects on labor demand can be found in H. Gregg Lewis, "Lecture Notes on the Demand for Labor" (manuscript, University of Chicago, 1974), p. 18. For the quantity of labor demanded to remain unchanged, the elasticity of labor efficiency (that is, the percentage increase in the ratio of output to labor inputs) to wages must equal the elasticity of labor demand divided by itself less one. For technological improvement to occur without a decline in labor demanded, the elasticity of labor demand must exceed unity. The resulting implied relative increase in efficiency will be large, exceeding unity, implying a lower price of output when wages are increased—a result not commonly observed.

conditions could the unlikely result of no disemployment occur. One of the conditions is that the price of output must be reduced and the demand for output must be sufficiently elastic to allow the effects of the labor-saving efficiencies to be offset by expanding sales. Given the varying sizes of past minimum-wage increases, it is difficult to believe that the "shock" of every increase fitted exactly into these necessary conditions and also matched exactly the corresponding alleged ineptitude of employers at the time of each increase.

The actual wages that employers will pay are determined by a number of factors. The simplest case to analyze is a competitive frictionless economy in which firms have no turnover costs. Assume, as throughout this section, that all workers have the same level of skill and are interchangeable. In this case, a cost-minimizing employer will try to pay the lowest wage possible that is still consistent with maintaining the work force he desires. His optimal wage will equal the workers' search income. Any lower wage will result in too many quits. Any higher wage will result in a surplus of applicants. This surplus of applicants signals the employer that his wage is too high relative to what he needs to pay to maintain his work force. Note, then, that it is the competition between workers, not between employers, that pushes wages down.

An issue that arises at this point is whether the level of unemployment in the absence of a minimum wage is good or bad from a social point of view. In a recent article I have developed a model of unemployment in which the level of unemployment in a free economy will be socially optimal in the absence of any unforeseen events.[8] The essential argument is that firms will pay a higher wage if the additional wage cost results in an even greater reduction elsewhere (for example, in turnover and supervision costs). To the degree that a firm pays in excess of the workers' search income, the extra pay will be a transfer from the firm to the worker that will, on the margin, cause more workers to seek the firm's jobs, so that the additional search costs of the unemployed will equal the additional wage costs. This additional cost is more than offset, however, by the

[8] For a dynamic rationing model of unemployment, see Walter J. Wessels, "The Contribution By Firms to Unemployment: A Dynamic Model," *Southern Economic Journal*, vol. 45, no. 4 (April 1979), pp. 1130–50. The model assumes that firms pay a wage in excess of search income so as to minimize turnover costs as well as to motivate workers and minimize supervision costs. An inventory model of unemployment, in which firms pay a wage in excess of search income so as to maintain a stock of available but unemployed workers, is presented in Robert B. Archibald, "Labor Queues and Involuntary Unemployment," *Economic Inquiry*, vol. 15, no. 1 (January 1977), pp. 33–50.

firm's reduction in other costs. At the optimal level of unemployment, the last additional dollar spent on wages (and thereby on search) results in a dollar reduction in the firm's other costs. At this level of unemployment, the economy has minimized the sum of its production and search costs. Any other level of unemployment will leave the economy worse off.

The analysis that follows ignores this form of unemployment for expositional simplicity and assumes instead that employers set their wages to equal the search income of their workers. Note, though, that in terms of the discussion (at the beginning of this chapter) of the minimum wage's effect on unemployment, it is only in the modified competitive labor market model with frictions that the existence of a minimum wage might lower unemployment. On the other hand, in the competitive frictionless labor market model, the introduction of a minimum wage will always increase unemployment, since there is no unemployment to begin with. In both models an *increase* in the minimum wage can either increase or decrease unemployment; it is this aspect of minimum wages that we are mainly concerned about empirically and to which we now turn.

Interpreting Changes in Unemployment

Unemployment is not only the state of being without a job but also the state of looking for employment. Unemployment and job search are thus understood here to be equivalent activities. We are thus ignoring, for expository simplicity, the existence of layoffs.

In the context of a competitive frictionless labor market model, there will be no unemployment, since wages will be pushed down by any surplus of job applicants, causing employers to increase employment until all surplus workers are absorbed. Workers will then be able to find work immediately without any job search. In equilibrium, wages will equal the search income of the marginal labor force participant, providing no incentive for any additional persons to enter the labor force.

When the existence of a minimum wage keeps wages from falling enough to employ all the persons seeking work, unemployment will result. Correspondingly, a divergence between wages and search income will also come about. These two variables, unemployment and the divergence between wages and search income, are interrelated. We will now describe this relationship.

Given the level of the minimum wage and the resulting level of employment, the number of jobs becoming available in any given period will be considered to be constant.[9] If these available job openings are rationed randomly among unemployed workers, as we shall assume, then an increase in the number of unemployed workers will reduce each worker's chance of finding a job within any given time. (Note that hereafter, when the phrase "the probability of getting a job" is used, we are referring to a given period and not to the probability of ever getting a job.) For example, if the number of persons unemployed doubles, the probability of getting a job should fall by half, and the resulting expected length of search should double.[10] An increase in unemployment will therefore reduce the probability of getting a job and will increase the expected length and thus the total expected costs of search. As a consequence, unemployment will be negatively related to search income.

In effect, in the presence of a minimum wage, unemployment replaces wages as the equilibrating mechanism that equates the demand for and supply of labor force participants. In the absence of a minimum wage, it is wages that fall to reduce search income to the level of the nonwork income of the marginal labor force participant. In the presence of the minimum wage, it is unemployment that increases to reduce search income. In particular, unemployment increases so as to reduce search income until employment plus unemployment equals the supply of labor force participants.

Having analyzed the components of the labor force, it is now possible to say how we can interpret changes in unemployment. By definition, labor force participation equals employment plus unemployment. Since a minimum-wage increase reduces employment, its effect on labor force participation (and thus on search income) depends on how it affects unemployment. If unemployment increases more than employment falls, obviously the number of the workers in the labor force has increased; this could only occur if the minimum wage had enhanced the search income of new entrants into the labor force. A higher search income will force employers not covered by the minimum wage to raise their wages so as to maintain their work force and ,will, of course, increase the welfare of the unemployed workers (which is measured by search income). Therefore a large increase in unemployment would imply that most workers are made

---

[9] We are assuming that the rate of turnover, γ, will remain constant. In fact, it may change. The effects of the change in γ are considered in Walter J. Wessels, *The Effects of Minimum Wages on the Youth Labor Market: An Expanded Model*, Technical Analysis Paper no. 66 (Washington, D.C.: U.S. Department of Labor, Office of the Assistant Secretary for Policy, Evaluation, and Research, July 1979), pp. 27–32.

[10] The expected length of search is inversely related to the probability of getting a job in a given period of search. As shown in footnote 5 of chapter 3, the expected number of searches equals $1/p$.

better off by the minimum wage. On the other hand, a decrease in unemployment or an increase smaller than the fall in employment implies that some workers are worse off, since search income must have declined when the labor force participation is smaller (as it is in this case). Employers not covered can lower their wages to match the lowered search income of their workers, and both uncovered workers and unemployed workers will be worse off.

Overall, the welfare effects of minimum wages are more readily ascertained from the changes in labor force participation (and should be positively related to these changes). Increases in unemployment are consistent with an improvement or a deterioration in the welfare of workers, whereas a decrease indicates that some workers, at least, are worse off. In the standard model, workers covered by the minimum wage are made better off if they can retain their jobs; in the expanded model, these workers will be made worse off when their search income is reduced, since employers can and will make enough offsets to lower the workers' utility to the level of their lowered search income.

The Effects of Minimum Wages in the Standard Model

In the standard model, employers do not make any nonwage offsets, so that workers in the jobs covered by the minimum wage enjoy the full increase in their money wages. Yet without offsets, the employers' costs are fully increased by the mandated wage increase, so that employment in covered jobs is reduced. A minimum-wage increase has, then, two main impacts: it makes minimum-wage jobs more valuable to workers, and it reduces the number of minimum-wage jobs. More workers will seek each minimum-wage job, since these jobs pay more than jobs not covered (at least, for workers of equal skill). There are fewer jobs, however, so that the net effect on the total number of workers who are unemployed (and seeking the minimum-wage jobs) is uncertain. In terms of the welfare of the work force, the central issue is whether labor force participation is increased or decreased or, equivalently, whether the number unemployed increases more or less than the drop in employment.

Suppose that initially, in a competitive frictionless economy, there is no unemployment and the jobs covered by the minimum wage pay the same wage as jobs not covered. Then a higher minimum wage is imposed. The number of covered minimum-wage jobs will decrease. Initially, however, the search income derived from seeking the minimum-wage jobs will be enhanced since these jobs pay more. Yet as more workers become unemployed so as to seek these jobs, each job will be rationed among the unemployed seeking it, and the expected waiting time and search costs needed to get a minimum-wage job will increase. The increase in unemployment will consequently reduce search income below the value of the minimum-wage job.

If the increase in unemployment is sufficiently large, search income and the size of the labor force will be reduced below their level before the minimum-wage increase. Those workers not covered by the minimum-wage law will be worse off because their employers will reduce their wages to match the workers' reduced search income. In addition, unemployed workers will obviously be worse off. On the other hand, when the increase in unemployment reduces search income below the value of the minimum-wage jobs but not below the search income existing before the minimum-wage increase (so that, on net, search income and the size of the labor force are increased), all workers will be better off. Those workers not covered will receive higher wages, and the unemployed will have a higher search income.

Now the central issue is, How much will search income be decreased? The answer depends on how much employment has fallen (for the more it falls, the more unemployment would have to be increased) and how much a given increase in unemployment reduces search income. The results in chapter 3 suggest that in the context of the standard model, for a reasonable range of parameters, search income should be increased. This implies that a minimum-wage increase should increase labor force participation. Yet in fact it does not. Past minimum-wage increases have reduced the labor force participation of most of the workers they have affected. This conflict between predicted and actual results suggests that the standard model may not be correct—employers may in fact make substantial offsets.

The Effects of Minimum Wages in the Expanded Model

In the expanded model, employers try to offset at least part of their higher mandated wage costs by making various offsets, such as those detailed in chapter 1, but the number of offsets they can make is limited. They cannot make so many offsets that the workers value their jobs less than their search income, for the workers will then quit. For example, we would expect a minimum-wage increase to reduce the safety of a job as employers reduced their expenditures on improving job safety. Yet it is highly improbable that these offsets would be so great that each worker would have a high chance of being killed.

When employers react to a minimum wage by trying to offset the higher wage costs, the net effect in the expanded model is a lowered utility for all workers and a reduced level of covered employment and labor force participation. In effect, the minimum wage acts as a tax on covered workers that forces them into uncovered jobs and out of the labor force.

The main effects of a minimum wage can be described with a simple example. Suppose that in a hypothetical labor market, workers buy for themselves a life insurance policy for $250. Now suppose employers find that they can offer the same policy at a cost to the employer of only $100. The initial employers offering this policy could ask their workers to accept as must as $250 in reduced wages, since workers would then be no better or worse off with or without the policy. These employers would profit by a reduced cost per worker of $150. Competition between employers would in the long run, however, bid the wage reduction down to the cost of the policy, $100, and workers would be better off by $150. Now suppose that a minimum wage is imposed, increasing each worker's wage by $180, and also suppose that each employer reacts by no longer offering the policy. Workers will be worse off by $70, gaining $180 in wages but losing $250 in fringe benefits. Employers are worse off by $80, saving $100 in fringe benefit costs but incurring $180 more in wage costs. Both employment and the labor supply in covered jobs will be reduced as a consequence, and if both of these reductions match, there will be no tendency for the labor market to change any further. The net effect of the minimum wage, then, is reduced employment in covered jobs and reduced full wages in all jobs.

This example illustrates the main factors that contribute to the negative outcome of the expanded model. First, workers pay for fringe benefits (and other nonwage benefits) by accepting wages that are lower than those that they would otherwise have received. Second, in the long run, the workers' wage reduction equals the employers' cost of providing the fringe benefits. Third, fringe benefit costs, except on the margin, are smaller than the value of the fringe benefits to the workers. As a result of these factors, when a minimum wage is imposed and employers reduce fringe benefits (and make other offsets) just enough to leave their workers' utility unchanged from its level before the minimum wage, the offset will be inadequate to offset fully the mandated increased wage costs. Employers will then cut back on employment, causing their disemployed workers to seek employment in uncovered jobs or to leave the labor force altogether. Employers not covered will reduce their wages to absorb the influx of workers; this lowered uncovered wage allows the covered employers to reduce the full wage of their workers by making even more offsets than initially, because their workers will not leave to take alternative jobs. In the expanded model the net result is that all workers, covered and not covered, are made worse off by minimum wages.

Summary

When the government imposes a price floor on buyers or a price ceiling on sellers, the buyers or sellers will try to offset their reduced profits by reducing the quality of what they are exchanging. For example, rent controls tend to reduce the quality of the apartments being offered as the owners offset their lower rental payments with reduced service and maintenance expenditures. Wage and price controls—for example, on gasoline prices—lead stores to be open fewer hours and to reduce the quality of what they sell by offering less service and by selling a poorer quality of goods. Similarly, minimum wages cause employers to reduce the quality of their jobs by making the offsets discussed in chapter 1. One consequence is that these offsets can be sufficient to make everyone worse off. Thus rent controls could lead to a lower utility for renters, and price controls could reduce the value that each dollar buys. In the case of minimum wages, workers in the jobs covered by the minimum wage could actually be made worse off by losing fringe benefits (and improved working conditions) that they valued more than their wage increase.

3

The Effects of Minimum Wages: A Graphic Analysis

This chapter presents a more detailed analysis of minimum wages, using graphs to illustrate its main points. These points were covered in chapter 2, and those without a sufficient training in economic analysis may want to turn to chapter 4 (which may be read without any loss in continuity). This chapter presents the standard model and then discusses the effects of minimum wages on fringe benefits, effort, and the hours of work. The expanded model is presented next. The chapter makes several novel points:

1. Because their welfare payments may be reduced if they earn a higher wage, workers on welfare will have a higher demand for fringe benefits and other positive nonwage aspects of their jobs. Correspondingly, a minimum-wage increase, by reducing their non-wage income, can harm these workers relatively more than workers not on welfare.

2. In the context of the expanded model, a minimum-wage increase can cause employers to increase the effort and hours of their workers to such a degree that output is increased and prices reduced—at the expense of the workers.

3. Also in the expanded model, if the demand-for-labor schedule is held constant, a greater reduction in employment implies a smaller reduction in the welfare of workers. When employment is unchanged, workers are worse off.

The Standard Model: A Graphic Presentation

The basic components of the labor force and their determinants were discussed in chapter 2. The size of the labor force is determined by the level of search income; the size of employment is determined

FIGURE 1
ONE-SECTOR STANDARD MODEL OF MINIMUM WAGES

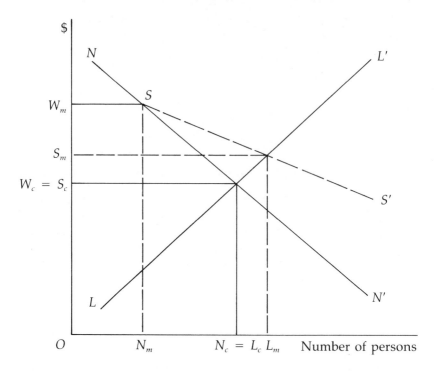

by the level of wages; and the size of unemployment is determined by how much unemployment is needed to equate search income to nonwork income.

These relationships are illustrated in figure 1. The horizontal axis is in units of persons and measures the size of employment and unemployment and the sum of these two, the size of the labor force. The vertical axis is in units of dollars and measures the level of search income (denoted as S) and wage income (denoted as W).

The supply schedule of labor force participants is represented by LL'. If search income is at S_c, for example, there will be L_c labor force participants, with the participant L_c having a nonwork income of S_c. At higher levels of search income, LL' shows that there are more labor force participants.

The demand for labor by employers is represented by NN'. At a wage of W_c, for example, employers will employ N_c workers. At higher wage levels, fewer workers will be employed, as NN' shows.

In the absence of a minimum wage, there will be no unemployment; wages will fall until there is a job opening for every job applicant. The equilibrium wage will occur when the demand for labor equals the supply of labor force participants. In figure 1, this occurs at the competitively determined wage W_c, where N_c workers are employed and the number of labor force participants is L_c. At this point, the market level of search income, S_c, equals the wage being paid, W_c.

Now suppose that a minimum wage of W_m is imposed on all employers. Firms will then reduce employment to N_m; but at N_m, wages exceed search income, so that there will be a surplus of labor force participants who will be unemployed.

To determine how many unemployed labor force participants there will be, it is necessary to construct a new schedule that relates search income to unemployment. This schedule is represented by SS'. This schedule begins at wage W_m and labor force participation level N_m; for if labor force participation were at this level, there would be no unemployment, and search income would equal the minimum wage. As the number of labor force participants is increased, unemployment increases, and search income falls (for with more unemployment, the probability of getting a job falls, and the expected length and costs of search increase). At higher levels of labor force participation, then, there will be correspondingly lower levels of search income; SS' is therefore shown to be negatively sloped. SS' is, in effect, the new demand schedule for labor force participants; it describes the potential search income that will exist for different levels of labor force participation.

This demand equals the supply of labor force participants at S_m. There will be, in equilibrium, N_m employed workers, L_m labor force participants, and $N_m L_m$ unemployed workers, as shown in figure 1.

In figure 1, all persons are shown to be made better off by a minimum-wage increase. The employed workers are obviously better off at their higher wage, but even the disemployed workers ($N_m N_c$) are better off, with a search income exceeding their previous wage. Similarly, the unemployed are better off, since their search income exceeds their prior wage or nonwage income. This result (that is, all workers are better off) occurs because the search income schedule (SS') was drawn with a less negative slope than that of the demand-for-labor schedule (NN'). It would have been equally possible, of course, to draw the search income schedule so that it was steeper than the demand-for-labor schedule. In this case, while the remaining employed workers would still have been made better off by a minimum-wage increase, the unemployed workers would have suffered, since their equilibrium search income would be lower than their previous competitive wage. (This is not shown, but the reader can verify it for himself by drawing SS' below NN'.) Jacob Mincer has developed a terminology to describe these two situations.[1] In the first case, where the minimum wage raised search income, we say that new labor force participants are "pulled" into the labor market to search for minimum-wage jobs. In the second case, where search income was reduced, some of the disemployed workers are "pushed" out of the labor market. The change in the net welfare of the disemployed workers thus depends on whether workers are pulled into or pushed out of the labor market.

A central issue in terms of the standard model is which schedule is steeper, the search income schedule or the demand-for-labor schedule. It is by this issue that the net change in search income and the welfare of disemployed workers is determined. Equivalently, the same issue determines whether a minimum wage increases or decreases labor force participation, and correspondingly, as can be seen from figure 1, the observed change in labor force participation can be used to judge how minimum wages affect search income and the welfare of the disemployed workers.

In this analysis, we have been considering the effects of the establishment of a minimum wage. The same analysis can be used to explore the effects of an increase in the minimum wage. An increase will shift the search income schedule back and raise the demand-for-labor schedule. When the search income schedule is less steep than the demand-for-labor schedule, a minimum-wage increase will result in an increase in search income, labor force participation, and unemployment. The welfare of all labor force participants will then be improved. On the other hand, when the search income schedule falls more than the demand-for-labor schedule, a minimum-wage increase will result in a decrease in search income and labor force participation. Unemployment may rise or fall, depending on which declines more—employment or labor force participation. The welfare of the disemployed workers will then be reduced.

In studying both the effects of the *existence* of a minimum wage and of an *increase* in a minimum wage, the central issue is whether the search income or the demand-for-labor schedule has a more negative slope. We will use this criterion to derive the predictions of the standard model. A major exception must now be noted, however. This occurs when the demand-for-labor schedule and the search income schedule are sloped as in figure 2. The imposition of

[1] Jacob Mincer, "Unemployment Effects of Minimum Wages," *Journal of Political Economy*, vol. 84, no. 4, pt. 2 (August 1976), supplement, pp. 87–104.

FIGURE 2
ONE-SECTOR STANDARD MODEL: A MAJOR EXCEPTION

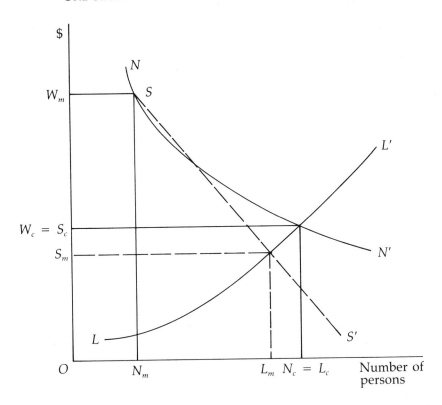

a minimum wage in this case results in a reduction in search income (from the competitive level where it equaled W_c to the new level of S_m). On the other hand, an increase in the minimum wage will raise search income above S_m, although it may still be below W_c.

Therefore, if we find that the demand-for-labor schedule is steeper than the search income schedule (as measured at N_m), we can only predict that an increase in the minimum wage will raise search income and thus labor force participation. It is not possible to infer in addition that the existence of a minimum wage has made workers better off in this case. Thus, if it were found that past minimum-wage increases had increased labor force participation, it could not be concluded that the existence of a minimum wage had made workers better off than they would have been without it. The only possible conclusion would be that workers were better off at higher minimum wages than they were at lower minimum wages.

From this analysis, especially of figure 1, we can see how the confounding of unemployment with disemployment has led to the wrong interpretation of the welfare implications of the unemployment changes caused by increases in the minimum wage. An increase in unemployment, being confused with an increase in disemployment, has been interpreted as implying that unemployed workers are worse off, when in fact no such interpretation is warranted, since an increase in unemployment is consistent with an increase or decrease in search income. A decrease in unemployment, far from being the positive effect it has been considered in the past, is in fact consistent only with a reduction in the welfare of the unemployed. In this context, it is interesting to note that the Bureau of Labor Statistics in a major report[2] on minimum wages has argued that minimum-wage increases have reduced the unemployment rate of several cohorts in the population, a position contrary to the bureau's notion that these increases in the minimum wage were not harmful to the unemployed.

A better measure of the welfare effects of minimum wages on the unemployed is the effects of the minimum wage on labor force participation. When a minimum-wage increase has increased labor force participation, it has increased search income. When it has reduced labor force participation, it has decreased search income. Labor force participation is thus a better measure of the effects of minimum wages than employment and unemployment, the two main variables on which most past minimum-wage studies have focused.

A Two-Sector Model

In the model presented above, all jobs were assumed to be covered by the minimum-wage provision of the Fair Labor Standards Act. In actual practice, however, a sizable number of jobs are not covered by minimum wages. The percentage of workers not covered in the private, nonagricultural sector of the economy has been declining, falling from 57 percent in 1938 to 16 percent in 1978. Some of the main workers not covered until recently have been retail trade and service workers, government workers, and domestic workers.

To incorporate the fact that some jobs are not covered by the minimum wage, we will now introduce an uncovered sector into our model. Because its wage will not be restrained by a minimum

---

[2] Hyman Kaitz, *Youth Unemployment and Minimum Wages*, Bureau of Labor Statistics Bulletin 1657 (Washington, D.C.: U.S. Department of Labor, 1970), chap. 2.

wage, this sector will act like the competitive frictionless labor market described. Employers not covered will react to a surplus of job applicants by reducing their wages and expanding their employment, with the result that in equilibrium there will be no unemployed workers in the uncovered sector of the economy. Once again, we could introduce various assumptions such that uncovered firms would permit a surplus of applicants and unemployment to exist. We will instead stay with the competitive frictionless labor market model described above, however, since its main implications are not likely to be altered radically by adding more assumptions to our model and it is the simplest model to present graphically.

Adding an uncovered sector to our model expands the options available to the workers disemployed by a minimum wage. In addition to leaving the labor force or being unemployed, they can now choose to work in the uncovered sector. Further, labor force participation is now made up of unemployment, employment in the covered sector, and employment in the uncovered sector. The number of labor force participants in the covered sector equals covered employment plus the total of unemployment (there is no unemployment in the uncovered sector because of its flexible wages). Correspondingly, the supply of labor force participants to the covered sector equals the difference between total labor force participation and employment in the uncovered sector. This supply is a positive function of search income; at higher search incomes there will be more labor force participants and fewer workers employed in the uncovered sector (the wage in that sector equals search income, and a higher wage results in less employment). The demand for labor force participants in the covered sector, given the level of the minimum wage, once again corresponds to the search income schedule. The resulting equilibrium value of search income occurs when the demand for and supply of labor force participants in the covered sector are equal. At this equilibrium value of search income, workers are indifferent between being unemployed and being employed in the uncovered sector.

The two-sector model of minimum wages is presented in figure 3. The demand for labor in the covered sector is represented by NN', which shows that fewer workers are employed in the covered sector at higher wages. LL' is the supply schedule of labor force participants, showing that there will be more participants at higher search incomes. $N_u N_u'$ is the demand-for-labor schedule in the uncovered sector when this demand is measured from right to left from the labor force participation schedule (LL'). For example, at a wage of W_c, the uncovered sector will employ $N_c L_c$ workers. $N_u N_u'$ is also the

FIGURE 3

TWO-SECTOR STANDARD MODEL OF MINIMUM WAGES

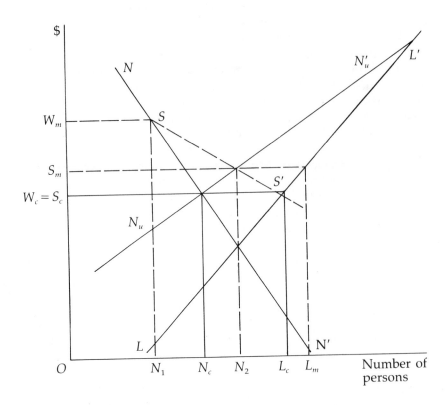

supply schedule of labor force participants to the covered sector
when this supply is measured from left to right from the vertical
axis. It shows the number of workers employed or looking for employment in the covered sector.

In the absence of a minimum wage, wages in both the covered
and the uncovered sectors will be bid down to the level of search
income, so that total employment equals total labor force participation and there is no unemployment. In figure 3, this occurs at
wage W_c and search income S_c, with N_c workers employed in the
covered sector and $N_c L_c$ workers in the uncovered sector.

The introduction of a minimum wage of W_m will reduce employment in the covered sector from N_c to N_1. The search income
schedule that relates the number of labor force participants in the
covered sector to the search income that would exist if the covered

sector's labor force participation equaled that number is shown by SS'. For example, if this number were N_1, search income would equal W_m, but as the number of unemployed workers increases, search income falls, as shown by the negative slope of the search income schedule, SS'.

SS' is also the demand schedule for covered-sector labor force participants. Since $N_u N'_u$ is the supply schedule of labor force participants in the covered sector, equilibrium occurs where demand equals supply at search income S_m. N_1 workers will be employed in the covered sector, and $N_2 L_m$ workers will be employed in the uncovered sector, the remaining labor force participants, $N_1 N_2$, being unemployed. The wage in the uncovered sector equals S_m, so that the unemployed workers are indifferent to a choice between unemployment and working in uncovered jobs.

In figure 3 the minimum wage is shown to increase the equilibrium value of search income. Both unemployed and uncovered workers are benefited by the minimum-wage increase, since their new income (equaling S_m) is higher. In effect, the minimum-wage increase has pulled workers from the uncovered sector and from outside the labor force into the covered sector. The wages of the workers not covered are bid up as their employers seek to prevent further attrition in their work force.

The unemployed workers and those not covered would instead have been made worse off had the search income schedule been drawn steeper than the demand-for-covered-labor schedule. The decrease in employment would then exceed the increase in unemployment, and some of the disemployed workers would be pushed into the uncovered sector, depressing wages there. The search income of the unemployed workers and the wages of the uncovered-sector workers would then be reduced as the uncovered employers lowered their wages to absorb the resulting surplus of workers seeking uncovered jobs. The effects of an increase in the minimum wage are determined by the same factors (that is, the relative slopes of SS' and NN') as the effects of the imposition of a minimum wage, with the exception noted in figure 2. The main difference between the analyses in figure 1 and figure 3 is that the supply of labor force participants to the covered sector is likely to be more elastic, ceteris paribus, when uncovered-sector employment is added as an option available to the disemployed workers. The effect of this more elastic schedule is that uncovered and unemployed workers will be affected less by a minimum-wage increase, being either helped less or harmed less.

The Effects of Minimum-Wage Increases

A central concern in the study of minimum-wage increases, in terms of their impact on the welfare of unemployed and uncovered workers, is whether the search income schedule has a more negative slope than the demand-for-covered-labor schedule. Note that only the slopes of these two schedules determine whether these workers will be made better or worse off by minimum-wage increase[3] (although, as shown in figure 2, we need to know more to determine whether the existence of a minimum wage has helped the uncovered and unemployed workers). The other schedules affect how much better off or worse off these workers will be but not whether a minimum-wage increase will make them better off or worse off.

We will seek to predict which schedule will be steeper by deriving an expression for search income. This derivation is presented in the appendix; the following are the main assumptions used to derive the expression for search income (these assumptions are somewhat standard in the search literature):

1. All job searchers have the same probability of getting a job in a given period (p), since the available job openings (A) are distributed randomly among the unemployed job searchers (U), so that $p = A/U$.

2. All workers have the same probability of losing their job within a given period (γ); this probability remains constant from period to period.

3. The labor market is stable, so that, given the level of the minimum wage, covered-sector employment (N) and the available number of jobs remain constant from period to period, with $A = \gamma N$.

4. All job searchers and workers face the same parameters in each period of search and work; these constant parameters include the minimum wage (W_m), nonwork income (W_o), and the full costs of search in a given period (C).

5. All persons work or search forever, never retiring from the labor market.

6. All persons are risk-neutral, valuing search income at its expected level.

None of these assumptions is truly realistic in our changing world, but it is believed that they approximate reality enough to render useful predictions. They can, of course, be modified; but

---

[3] An implicit assumption in our discussion is that no two of the various possible SS' schedules at various levels of the minimum wage will intersect.

since many of the modifications do not radically affect the results derived from these simplifying assumptions, most of them will not be considered. One assumption that will be modified because it does affect the results is the fifth, that workers work "forever." For a few years of work, this assumption does not distort our results; but because some workers may plan to work at minimum-wage jobs for only a short time, this assumption will have to be modified. The sixth assumption has been questioned by King;[4] if workers are risk-averse, the value of a minimum-wage increase will be reduced by the increased variance in income it may produce. Since it is difficult to ascertain whether low-wage workers are risk-averse or the degree to which they are, this modification will not be considered.

In addition, we assume that the labor market operates in "periods" of time such that in each period unemployed workers make one job search. At the end of each period, job searchers find out if they have been hired, and workers find out if they have been terminated from their jobs. Under these conditions, the following expression for search income is derived in the appendix:

$$S = \frac{pW_m + (r + \gamma)(W_o - C)}{p + r + \gamma} \tag{2}$$

where r is the interest rate. For the marginal labor force participant, whose search income equals his nonwork income, we will have, by letting $W_o = S$,

$$\frac{W_m - S}{r + \gamma} = \frac{C}{p} \tag{3}$$

Expression (3) can be interpreted as follows. The expected number of searches is the reciprocal of p,[5] so that the expected total of search cost equals C/p. The right-hand side is then the expected total costs of search. The left-hand side is the present expected value of the gain from acquiring a minimum-wage job—each period's gain, $W_m - S$, when divided by $(r + \gamma)$, yields the present expected value of this gain. The marginal worker, in this context, is indifferent to a choice between the total expected search costs and the total expected gains from searching for a minimum-wage job.

---

[4] Allan G. King, "Minimum Wages and the Secondary Labor Market," *Southern Economic Journal*, vol. 41, no. 2 (October 1974), pp. 215–19.

[5] If a job searcher has a probability "p" of getting a job in any given period of search, then his expected number of searches will be $p + (1 - p)p2 + (1 - p)^2 p3 + \ldots$ This expression follows because each possible number of searches is weighted by the probability that exactly that number will occur. Letting EN equal the sum of this series, subtract $(1 - p)EN$ from it. The resulting expression will be $pEN = p[1 + (1 - p) + (1 - p)^2 + \ldots]$, or $pEN = 1$, or $EN = 1/p$. The expected number of searches (EN) therefore equals the reciprocal of p.

The probability of getting a job, using assumptions 1 and 3, equals

$$p = \gamma N / U \qquad (4)$$

As can be seen from expression (4), an increase in unemployment will reduce the probability of getting a job. Combining expression (3) with expression (4) and solving for S in terms of U gives the following expression for the search income schedule:

$$S = W_m - \frac{(r + \gamma)C}{\gamma N} U \qquad (5)$$

The slope of the search income curve equals those terms preceding U. Higher search costs, lower employment in the covered sector, higher interest rates, and lower turnover rates will all cause this schedule to have a steeper slope.

If the elasticity of the demand for covered labor (stated in absolute terms) is η, then the slope of the demand schedule for covered labor will be:

$$- \frac{W_m}{N} \frac{1}{\eta} \qquad (6)$$

The smaller the elasticity, the steeper will be the slope of this schedule.

As stated at the beginning of this section, a central issue is which schedule—the demand-for-covered-labor schedule or the search income schedule—will have a more negative slope. All workers will be made better off by a minimum-wage increase, and labor force participation will be increased as a result, when the demand for covered labor has the more negative slope. This will occur when:

$$\eta_c < \frac{\gamma}{r + \gamma} \frac{W_m}{C} \qquad (7)$$

We will now use this expression to estimate the likely effects of a minimum-wage increase.

The right-hand term, in all likelihood, exceeds unity in value. The cost of a period of search C includes both the explicit and direct costs of searching for work and the implicit time costs. Stephenson, in a survey of teen-agers, found that their direct costs of search were usually less than ten dollars a week.[6] A survey by the Department of Labor found that most job searchers spent less than ten hours a

---

[6] S. P. Stephenson, Jr., "The Economics of Youth Job Search Behavior," *Review of Economics and Statistics*, vol. 58, no. 1 (February 1976), pp. 104–11.

week in search.[7] If this time were valued at the minimum wage and if time costs were the only costs of search, then W_m/C would equal four for a minimum-wage job of forty hours a week (note that W_m is the minimum-wage income for the "period," here a week, that we are considering). The addition of the ten-dollar-a-week direct cost would change this ratio to 2.7 (using the minimum wage in 1975, when Stephenson's survey was made). A lower bound for W_m/C of two would therefore seem reasonable. The annual turnover rate in minimum-wage jobs (as reflected in γ) seems likely to exceed the annual rate of interest, making the first term on the right-hand side, $\gamma/(r + \gamma)$, exceed 0.5 in value. For example, if one-third of the workers change jobs annually (which is close to the national average) and the interest rate is 10 percent, this expression has a value of 0.77. Using these values, we obtain a lower-bound value for the right-hand side of 1.0, with a more likely value of 2.1 (derived by multiplying 2.7 by 0.77).

If we now consider the right-hand side of expression (7), most estimates of the elasticity of labor demand are below unity. For example, Clark and Freeman estimated an elasticity of labor demand that, though significantly higher than those previously estimated in the economic literature, had a value of only 0.5.[8] Philip Cotterill estimated the elasticity of labor demand for low-wage industries to be near 0.8.[9]

Most estimates of the elasticity of labor demand with respect to minimum-wage increases are also small, usually below 0.2. The main exceptions are Zucker (who found an elasticity of demand for workers of 1.01 and for man-hours of 1.15), Reynolds and Gregory (who found values of 1.1 for 1949–1954 and 0.92 for 1954–1958 in Puerto Rico), and Lianos (who found a value of 1.1 for agricultural employment and a value of 3.51 for one region in the long run).[10]

Even with these higher estimates and certainly with the average

---

[7] U.S. Department of Labor, *1973 Job Finding Survey*, Special Report, Washington, D.C., August 1974.

[8] Kim B. Clark and Richard B. Freeman, *How Elastic Is the Demand for Labor?* National Bureau of Economic Research Working Paper no. 309 (Cambridge, Mass., January 1979).

[9] Philip Cotterill, "The Elasticity of Demand for Low-Wage Labor," *Southern Economic Journal*, vol. 41, no. 3 (January 1975), pp. 520–25.

[10] Albert Zucker, "Minimum Wages and the Long-Run Elasticity of Demand for Labor," *Quarterly Journal of Economics*, vol. 87, no. 2 (May 1973), pp. 267–77; Lloyd G. Reynolds and Peter Gregory, *Wages, Productivity, and Industrialization in Puerto Rico* (Homewood, Ill.: Richard D. Irwin, 1965); and Theodore P. Lianos, "Impact of Minimum Wages upon the Level and Composition of Agricultural Employment," *Southern Economic Journal*, vol. 54, no. 3 (August 1972), pp. 477–84. A central limitation of these estimates, in the context of the expanded model, is that the change in employment reflects a shift not along the demand schedule for covered labor because of higher wages but rather in the supply of labor because of lower full wages.

lower estimates found in almost every other study, the inequality in expression (7) holds; the standard model of minimum wages therefore predicts that a minimum-wage increase will increase search income and labor force participation. Using a similar model, Gramlich derived the same prediction for most cohorts in our society (the exception being teen-agers).[11] As we shall see in chapter 4, this prediction of the standard model is wrong.

In the analysis above, it was assumed that workers work at (or search for) minimum-wage jobs "forever." For teen-agers seeking summer employment and for workers who plan to earn lower wages for a short time, this is an unrealistic assumption. The effect of modifying this assumption is to reduce the present value of the benefits of a minimum-wage increase as workers are in minimum-wage jobs for a shorter period of time. If we assume instead that job searchers work for n periods, then condition (7) can be written as

$$\eta < a\gamma\frac{W_m}{C} \tag{8}$$

where a is the present value of one dollar paid out for n periods (the derivation of this expression is presented in the appendix). For an annual interest rate of 10 percent and an n of 52 weeks, a equals 49.6. For the average value of the parameters described above (W_m/C equaling 2.7 and γ annually equaling 0.33), the right-hand side of expression (8) then has a value of 0.74 (note that γ as well as r must be expressed in terms of weeks). This value exceeds most estimates of the elasticity of labor demand, and thus this modification does not change the prediction of the standard model that a minimum-wage increase should increase labor force participation. For a summer job (of, let us say, ten weeks' duration), the right-hand side has a value of 0.15, so that a minimum-wage increase would be predicted by the standard model to reduce the labor force participation of summer workers (unless turnover in summer jobs is substantially larger).

Another modification would be to consider part-time workers, whose W_m/C value should be smaller. For example, if minimum-wage jobs are twenty, not forty, hours a week, then when part-time workers spend the same time and costs in search as full-time workers, the values of the right-hand side would be halved. This suggests that a minimum-wage increase will have a smaller positive effect for part-time workers who are not employed and not covered, and may in some cases have a negative effect.

[11] Edward M. Gramlich, *Impact of Minimum Wages on Other Wages, Employment and Family Income*, Brookings Papers on Economic Activity, no. 2 (Washington, D.C.: Brookings Institution, 1976), pp. 409–51.

Another aspect of minimum-wage increases not yet considered is that their short-run effects may differ from their long-run effects. At the time of the increase, employers will be cutting back on their labor force, so that the relative availability of jobs (as reflected in γ) should fall, making the short-run effects of the increase more negative than its long-run effects on labor force participation.

Summary of the Standard Model

In this analysis we have developed a model of minimum wages that describes the effects of a minimum-wage increase when employers do not make any of the offsets described in chapter 1. In this model, an increase in the minimum wage increases the value of being unemployed by raising the value of covered jobs, but it also decreases the value of being unemployed by reducing the availability of jobs. When the first factor predominates, the expected search income of unemployed workers will be increased by a minimum-wage increase, pulling workers from uncovered jobs and from outside the labor force into the search for minimum-wage jobs. Wages in the uncovered jobs will rise as a consequence; all workers are then benefited by the minimum-wage increase, including those disemployed by it. When the second factor predominates, the expected search income of unemployed workers falls, pushing some of the disemployed workers into uncovered jobs or out of the labor force. Wages in the uncovered sector will be reduced, with the result that both unemployed and uncovered workers are harmed by the minimum-wage increase.

A main variable permitting us to judge which of these two effects on search income predominates is labor force participation. The change in labor force participation is likely to be positively related to the net change in search income caused by a minimum-wage increase. As a variable it is preferable to unemployment—a variable widely used in past studies. An increase in unemployment can be associated with either an increase or a decrease in search income, and its use has, as a consequence no implications for the welfare effects of minimum-wage increases. On the other hand, a decrease in unemployment can only be associated with a decrease in search income, implying that the workers not employed or not covered have been harmed. This implication opposes the usual interpretation of this change in the minimum-wage literature.

The principal prediction derived from the standard model is that a minimum-wage increase should increase labor force participation. Although the matter is not explicitly discussed in this chapter, the standard model also clearly predicts that a minimum-wage increase should reduce the quit rate of covered jobs and raise the costs of covered employers. These predictions are tested in chapter 4.

The Expanded Model

The remainder of this chapter may be outlined as follows. We will first investigate the demand for and supply of fringe benefits and then describe how a minimum wage will affect fringe benefits. We will do the same next for the demand for and supply of effort and finally for the hours of work. Each of these offsets will be treated separately, as if each were the only one employers made, although of course all types of offsets may be made simultaneously. For each offset, we will discuss how the cost of minimum wages will be shared between employers and workers and also the ultimate effect on the welfare of workers in the context of the two-sector minimum-wage model.

Before describing how these offsets affect the welfare of workers, however, it is necessary to introduce a new term into our discussion: the monetarized value of the utility that a worker gets from his job will be referred to as his "full wage." A worker's full wage is the sum of his after-tax money wage plus the monetary value he places on the fringe benefits he receives, on his working conditions, on his work effort, on his hours of work, and on the many other aspects involved in his job. Once we consider these nonwage aspects of work, full wages replace money wages in our description of the model of the competitive labor market. When workers are all equally skilled and have the same tastes, they will receive the same full wage (not money wage) in all jobs within the competitive frictionless labor market. Cost minimization by employers and competition between workers will cause the full wage in all jobs to be equal to the level of search income that equates total employment with total labor force participation. The introduction of a minimum wage is not assumed to alter this result; the only difference is that covered employers will *reduce* the positive nonwage aspects of their jobs until their workers' full wage equals their search income. We will now explore the first of the offsets and its resulting effects.

Fringe Benefits: Demand and Supply

Fringe benefits will be defined as any positive aspect of work other than wages on which the employer makes expenditures. They include not only such conventional items as pensions or life and health insurance but also such items as safe working conditions, considerate management, and a pleasant working environment. A particularly important fringe benefit from the viewpoint of the workers' welfare is on-the-job training.

A worker pays for fringe benefits by accepting a greater differential between what he produces and what he is paid. We will refer to this wider differential as "a reduction in wages," although it could have come about from greater effort. (The effects of effort are considered in the next section.)

In supplying fringe benefits to their workers, employers seek to provide at the lowest cost possible a full wage equal to their workers' search income. Employers will consequently be willing to spend an additional dollar on fringe benefits as long as money wages can then be reduced by a dollar or more, assuming that the workers' full wage does not fall below their search income. The worker, in turn, is willing to reduce his money wages as long as his full wage is increased or left unchanged. At the employer's lowest cost per worker, given the worker's full wage, the marginal dollar spent on fringe benefits and on money wages should both increase the worker's full wage by the same amount. The effect of a minimum wage is to restrain the worker from accepting lower wages in exchange for the fringe benefits he wants. Therefore, in this case, the marginal dollar spent on fringe benefits will be more valued than that spent on money wages: the value of fringe benefits to the workers will exceed their cost to the employer. A minimum-wage increase, when offset by an equal reduction in fringe benefits, will thus result in the loss of fringe benefits valued at more than their cost and thereby at more than the increase in wages. The net result will be a reduction in the worker's full wage. This result is ultimately responsible for the predicted negative effects of minimum wages in the expanded model.

Figure 4 shows the demand for and supply of fringe benefits for a representative employer. The demand schedule (DD') shows the maximum wage reduction a worker will accept for each additional unit of fringe benefit, given the quantity of fringe benefits with which he has already been supplied. If the worker were actually charged these amounts, his full wage would be the same, no matter what quantity he was supplied. For example, the worker is willing to pay up to OA in lower wages to acquire unit O_c of fringe benefits; any higher price will lower his full wage. To construct the supply schedule, the units of fringe benefits will be defined so that each unit costs the same amount for the employer to supply. If these units are made up of different compositions of fringe benefits, we shall also assume that the employer supplies the most demanded

FIGURE 4
FRINGE BENEFITS: DEMAND AND SUPPLY

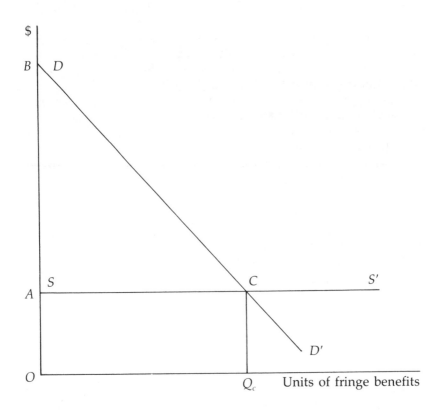

units first. These assumptions are made to simplify our exposition and do not affect our results in any way. Because of the way the units of fringe benefits have been defined, the supply schedule (SS') of fringe benefits will be horizontal, each unit costing the employer OA to supply. The supply schedule shows the smallest wage reduction the employer will accept to supply each unit of fringe benefits.

If there were only one employer in the labor market supplying fringe benefits, he could ask workers to reduce their wages by the full amount shown by the demand schedule. The firm would then reduce its per worker cost (wage cost plus fringe-benefit cost) by supplying an additional unit of fringe benefits as long as the resulting wage reduction exceeded the cost of that unit of fringe benefit. At the optimal quantity of fringe benefits, where its per worker cost will be minimized, the last or marginal unit of fringe benefit will yield a wage reduction just equal to the firm's cost for that unit. In terms of figure 4, the amount of fringe benefits that a cost-minimizing employer will want to supply is Q_c. If it were to supply any more units beyond Q_c, its resulting wage reductions would be inadequate to cover the costs of the additional fringe benefits, increasing its cost per worker. As long as it is the sole employer offering fringe benefits, this employer could ask for and get a wage reduction equal to the area of $OBCQ_c$; this total wage reduction (which equals the sum of the wage reductions workers are willing to accept for each of the units of fringe benefit) will leave their workers as well off as they were without the fringe benefits. Since the cost of supplying these units equals the area $OACQ_c$, this employer's resulting profit and net cost reduction equals area ABC.

When there is competition from other employers, though, these profits will be bid away as competing employers bid down the wage reductions they demand as they try to hire more workers to profit from. In the long run, when all profits are bid away, the worker's wage reduction will be bid down to the employer's cost of supplying the fringe benefits. The differential between the worker's productivity and his wages will be $OACQ_c$. What was formerly the employer's profit will now become the consumer's surplus enjoyed by the worker, so that area ABC represents an addition to his utility and full wages. Although employers are not making any profit, any attempt to reduce fringe benefits below Q_c will result in a higher cost per worker because they will have to raise their wages more than their fringe-benefit costs are reduced to maintain their workers' full wage level at the market level of search income.

The effect of a minimum wage is to prevent workers from exchanging lower wages for more valued fringe benefits. To illustrate the net effect of a minimum wage on the full wages of workers and the costs of employers, we will present two extreme cases that bound the possible consequences of a minimum-wage increase in the expanded model. In the first extreme case, the supply of labor force participants to the covered sector is perfectly inelastic, so that the same number of persons are willing to be employed or unemployed in that sector at any full wage and search income (graphically this is shown by a perfectly vertical supply schedule). As we shall show, in this extreme case the workers bear the full costs of the minimum-wage increase. In the second extreme case, the supply of covered labor force participants is perfectly elastic, so that no person will accept a full wage or search income below the competitively determined level (graphically this is shown by a perfectly horizontal supply schedule). In this case the employer bears the full cost of the minimum-wage increase. The actual outcome of a minimum-wage increase will probably fall between these two extreme cases, the worker and employer sharing the costs.

The first extreme case, to repeat, assumes that the supply of labor force participants who are covered is perfectly inelastic. We will assume that initially, before the minimum wage is imposed, employers are supplying the optimal quantity of fringe benefits at no profit to themselves. In addition, we assume that employers are cost minimizers, so that they will keep their workers' full wage at the market level of search income. Any lower full wage will result in quits, and any higher full wage is an unnecessary cost. The effect of an imposition of a minimum wage will be analyzed in three stages. These stages are for expository purposes only; no temporal sequence of events is implied by the sequence of stages. In the first stage, employers are assumed to reduce their fringe benefits only enough to keep their workers' full wage at its previous competitive level. That is, the workers' value of the eliminated fringe benefits will equal the value of their mandated increased wages, and the value of the workers' increased wages will equal the employers' increased wage costs.

Yet because the cost of the eliminated fringe benefits is *less* than their value to the worker and because their value (in the first stage) equals the increased wage costs, it follows that, in the first stage, the reduced fringe-benefit cost will be smaller than the increased wage cost. In the first stage, then, the employer has a higher total cost per worker, and the worker has an unchanged full wage. In the second stage, the employer is assumed to try to reduce his employment in response to his higher first-stage cost per worker. The attempted reduction in employment lowers the availability of jobs and thereby lowers the search income of workers. With the lower search income, the employer, in the third stage, can make still further offsets as he lowers his workers' full wage to their new, lower search income. In the first extreme case, workers in the covered sector are willing to accept any lower value of search income as long as their employment is not reduced. Therefore employers can fully offset all minimum-wage costs by reducing their fringe-benefit expenditures by an amount equal to their higher wage costs. Employment will not be reduced, but workers will have a lower full wage, bearing the full costs of the minimum-wage increase.

The effects of a minimum wage in the first extreme case can be illustrated by figure 5. Assume that the minimum wage raised the employer's costs by an area equal to Q_mFCQ_c. The employers can

48

FIGURE 5
EFFECTS OF MINIMUM WAGES ON FRINGE BENEFITS

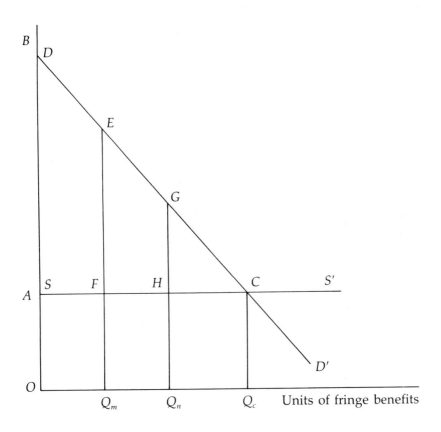

fully offset these costs in this case by cutting back fringe-benefit costs an equal amount, reducing the level of fringe benefits from the competitive level Q_c to the smaller level Q_m. Workers gain area Q_mFCQ_c in increased wages but lose fringe benefits they valued at Q_mECQ_c. Their net loss is area FEC, their lost consumer's surplus. Because of the inelastic supply of covered labor force participants, employers can pass the full cost of the minimum-wage increase to their workers, who must bear these costs in lower full wages and search income. Employers in the uncovered sector can then reduce their full wages to the lowered value of search income, so that all workers are made worse off by the minimum-wage increase.

The second extreme case assumes that the supply of covered labor force participants is perfectly elastic. Employers in this case cannot lower their workers' full wage; if they did so, they would lose their entire work force. In terms of the three stages, we will now only have the first two stages. Employers will make just enough offsets to keep their workers at the competitively determined level of full wages. Since employers will then have a higher net cost per worker, they will cut back on employment until the marginal productivity of workers rises enough to cover the cost of the minimum-wage increase. Employment will be reduced, but search income and full wages will remain unaffected.

The effects of a minimum-wage increase in the second extreme case can also be illustrated by figure 5. The employer, in seeking to maintain his worker's full wage at its original level, will reduce fringe benefits only so much that the lost value to the worker equals the amount his money wages have been increased. In figure 5, a minimum wage that imposes a higher wage cost equal to area Q_nGCQ_c is needed to cause employers to reduce their fringe benefits from Q_c to Q_n. Their wage cost is increased by Q_nGCQ_c, and their fringe-benefit cost is reduced only by area Q_nHCQ_c, so that their net cost per worker is increased by area HCG. It is the employer, then, who bears the cost of the minimum wage in this case. Workers are neither benefited nor harmed by the minimum wage.

The actual results of a minimum wage (in the expanded model) are likely to be between these two cases. In the first stage, employers make enough offsets to maintain their workers' full wage at its initial level. In the second stage, their higher cost per worker will cause them to cut back on employment, with the result that in the third stage they can make still further offsets, since workers will have a reduced search income because of their reduced covered employment. If the supply of labor to the covered sector is not perfectly inelastic, the employer will not be able to offset the costs of the minimum-wage increase fully and instead will have to reduce employment; if the supply of labor is not perfectly elastic, workers will suffer a lowered full wage as covered employment is reduced. Employment and labor force participation will be reduced, with employers and workers sharing the net costs of the minimum-wage increase (that is, they will share the costs of losing area FEC).

The worker's ultimate share of the net cost of the minimum-wage increase is determined by several factors. As is obvious from the foregoing analysis, his share will be smaller, ceteris paribus, the more elastic the supply schedule of covered labor force participants is or, equivalently, the more elastic the supply of labor force participation to the whole labor market is and the more elastic the demand for labor by employers who are not covered. In addition, in terms of figure 5, these costs will be smaller, the smaller area *FEC* is. The worker's reduction in full wages will thus be smaller, the more elastic his demand for fringe benefits is. Finally, the covered employers will be able to bear more of the cost of the minimum-wage increase, the more inelastic their demand schedule for workers is.

One consideration not mentioned so far is the effect of taxes on the worker's loss from minimum wages. Most taxes, including the income tax, are imposed on money wages and not on most fringe benefits. Taxes thus act as a subsidy to fringe benefits, by giving an incentive to employers and workers to shift expenditures from where they are taxed, that is, from wages, to where they are not taxed, or to fringe benefits. At a marginal tax rate of t, a dollar reduction in before-tax wages becomes only a $(1 - t)$ dollar reduction in after-tax wages. For example, at a tax rate of 30 percent, if the employer reduced wage costs by ten dollars, the worker's after-tax income would be reduced by only seven dollars. Alternatively stated, the worker needs to pay, in terms of *his* reduced after-tax wages, only seven dollars for a fringe benefit that costs the employer ten dollars.

Taxes, then, reduce the effective cost to workers of purchasing fringe benefits. In terms of figures 4 and 5, the effective supply schedule to the worker is below *SS'*, each unit costing the worker only $(1 - t)OA$ to buy. Obviously the effect of taxes is to increase the relative amount of fringe benefits that the workers will demand and that will be supplied. As a result, the employers will be able to offset larger minimum-wage increases through this type of offset. On the other hand, a minimum wage may have some social benefit (offsetting some of its losses), since it reduces the number of fringe benefits supplied to workers that are valued below their social cost. It is possible that some size of minimum-wage increases may, in a second-best sense, be socially efficient, although this approach to raising the social welfare would probably be quite uncertain in its effects, as well as being considered perverse and inequitable by many persons.

Our consideration of taxes may be regarded as superfluous in the context of minimum wages, since low-wage workers are not usually in high tax brackets. Still, many low-wage workers receive welfare payments that may be reduced if they earn more, these reductions acting as an effective tax on money wages. The implicit tax rate, for example, of the Aid to Families with Dependent Children program averaged 65 percent in 1967 and 37 percent in 1971.[12] The

---

[12] Robert M. Hutchens, "Changes in AFDC Tax Rates in 1967–71," mimeographed (Madison: Institute for Poverty Research, University of Wisconsin, July 1976).

maximum rates were 86 percent and 58 percent in the same years. Given this high rate of implicit subsidy for fringe benefits, workers affected by these programs will have had a substantially increased demand for fringe benefits and will therefore have had a larger consumer's surplus that could have been reduced by minimum wages. In terms of figure 5, the effective cost to these workers of fringe benefits will be reduced, since lower wages will result in higher welfare payments. As in the case of taxes, these workers will demand more fringe benefits. Unlike workers in the tax case, however, these workers will lose more when minimum wages are increased: they will lose the same amount of fringe benefits, but they will also suffer from reduced welfare payments. Thus it is the workers on welfare who will be most harmed by minimum wages.

Effort: Demand and Supply

Just as there is a demand for and a supply of work time, there is a demand for and a supply of work effort. Although effort is a somewhat ambiguous concept, we will assume that those components of effort relevant to employers can be measured in some type of units. The demand by employers for these units of effort is derived from the fact that each additional unit raises the worker's productivity. From these increases in productivity, the employer may have to subtract any additional supervisory costs he must take on to make certain that the extra effort he demands is forthcoming. A demand schedule for effort will then show the increased productivity due to each additional unit of effort net of additional supervisory costs; these net increases in productivity would be expected to become smaller as more effort is demanded, so that the demand schedule is negatively sloped. The supply by workers of the units of effort reflects their forgone value, since they could be used elsewhere for direct enjoyment. Because workers will give up the least valued units of effort to their employer first, each additional unit has a higher and higher cost. In the absence of a minimum wage, the optimal amount of effort, which maximizes the employer's profit in the short run and the worker's full wage in the long run, occurs when the net gain of the marginal unit to the employer equals the monetary value of the additional sacrifice the worker must make to supply it. The introduction of a minimum wage encourages the employer to demand even more effort than this amount, and as in the fringe-benefit case, workers will be made worse off by the minimum wage.

Figure 6 illustrates the demand for and supply of effort. DD' represents the demand schedule of employers for effort; it shows their net gain from each additional unit. The gain from unit Q_m is,

52

FIGURE 6
EFFORT: DEMAND AND SUPPLY

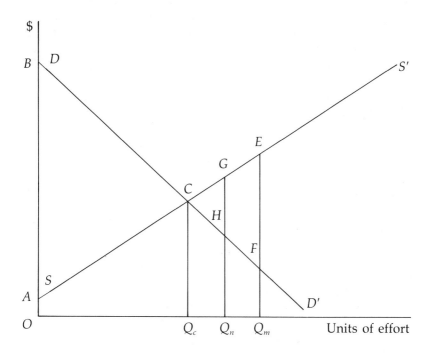

for example, Q_mF. SS' represents the supply schedule by workers of effort; it shows the forgone cost of supplying each additional unit. The cost of unit Q_m to the worker is, for example, Q_mE. The optimal amount of effort is Q_c. In the short run, the employer will make a profit of ABC by demanding this amount, compensating workers $OACQ_c$ while gaining $OBCQ_c$ in increased productivity net of supervisory costs. In the long run, though, the worker will receive the full value of his effort in higher wages, gaining $OBCQ_c$ in increased wages for supplying effort costing him only $OACQ_c$, for a net surplus of ABC. We will now use figure 6 to illustrate the effects of a minimum wage when the employer responds by demanding more effort; we will employ the same two extreme cases as we did for fringe benefits.

In the first extreme case, labor force participation in the covered sector is assumed to be perfectly inelastic. In the first stage, when a minimum wage is imposed, the employer increases only the extra amount of effort he demands, so that the worker's full wage is not reduced below its initial competitive level. Since the net gain to the

53

employer from this extra effort is less than its costs to the worker and the cost to the worker equals his higher wages (since the full wage is assumed to be left unchanged in the first stage), the employer will not be able to offset all the higher wage costs due to the minimum wage in the first stage. He will thus cut back on employment in the second stage, reducing the search income of workers and allowing him to demand more effort and give his workers lower full wages in the third stage. Because workers will accept any lower full wage (in the first extreme case) to maintain their initial level of employment, the employer can demand enough effort to offset his higher mandated money wage costs fully. Employment will not be reduced, but the full wage of all workers will be decreased by the minimum wage, since they bear all of its costs.

The net outcome of this first case can be illustrated by figure 6. Employers can fully offset a minimum-wage increase that increases wages Q_cCFQ_m by increasing effort from Q_c to Q_m. Their net gains from the increased effort then offset their higher wage costs. Their workers will be worse off, however; their wages are increased by Q_cCFQ_m, but the extra effort costs them Q_cCEQ_m, so that their full wages are reduced by CEF.

In the second extreme case, the supply of covered labor force participation is perfectly elastic, so that employers cannot lower the full wage of their workers without losing their whole work force. Only the first two stages will be relevant, then, the increase in wages equaling the cost to the worker of the extra effort he must make. In terms of figure 6, it will take a minimum-wage increase of Q_cCGQ_n to increase effort to Q_n in this second case. The employer's wage cost of Q_cCGQ_n is only partially offset by a net increase in productivity of Q_cCHQ_n, so that its net cost is increased by CHG. Employment will then be reduced, but the worker's full wage will be unchanged.

In the intermediate cases between these extremes, employers and workers will share the cost of the minimum-wage increase, with a consequential reduction in employment and full wages. The worker's loss will be greater, ceteris paribus, the larger the area CEF is; therefore the worker's loss will be greater, the more inelastic the demand for effort is and the more inelastic its supply.[13]

Hours of Work: Demand and Supply

Certain employers who are affected by a minimum-wage increase may find it to their advantage to change their hours of work, to the

---

[13] An exception to this proposition occurs when the demand for effort is sufficiently inelastic that the firm will not increase effort beyond some point.

FIGURE 7

HOURS OF WORK WHEN HOURLY PRODUCTIVITY VARIES BY HOURS
WORKED

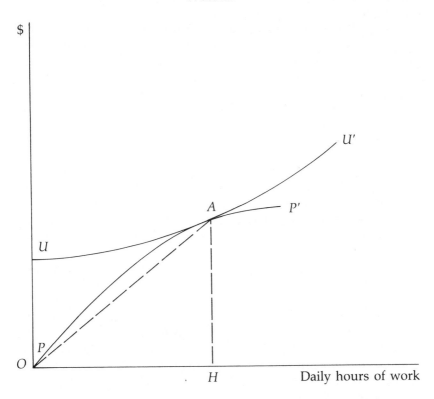

possible detriment of their workers.[14] As is clear from chapter 1, this is one of the main ways retail stores have adjusted to minimum-wage increases, and therefore this form of adjustment merits attention. This section is more technical, and the reader who does not have an extensive economics background may wish to go to the next section.

We will first discuss a case where employers react to a minimum wage by reducing their workers' hours of work. We will assume that their workers' marginal product varies from hour to hour during a day.[15] Since in a competitive market these employers will not make

---

[14] See J. Wilson Mixon, *The Minimum Wage and the Job Package*, Bureau of Labor Statistics, Working Paper 32 (Washington, D.C.: U.S. Department of Labor, January 1975), pp. 8–15, for a discussion related to the one presented here.

[15] This analysis applies equally as well to hours per day, hours (or weeks) per year, and years per lifetime.

any profit in the long run, their daily costs per worker must equal the worker's daily productivity; it follows that in some hours workers produce more than their hourly wages, while in other hours they produce less.

Figure 7 illustrates this case. The vertical axis shows the daily income and productivity of workers, while the horizontal axis shows the daily hours of work. UU' is the worker's utility schedule; he is indifferent to a choice between the set of hours of work and the daily incomes it shows. UU' is chosen to correspond to the competitive level of full wages existing before a minimum wage. The worker will be better off with any position to the northwest, since he prefers more income and fewer hours of work. The increasing slope of UU' shows that the worker's relative dislike of working increases as he works more hours, so that he needs increasing additions to his income to compensate him for working more and more hours if his full wage is to remain unchanged. PP' shows the daily output of workers when they work various hours of work; the employer is assumed to employ them during the most productive hours first, so that PP' increases at a decreasing rate as less productive hours are added. Hours H shows a competitive market equilibrium, where the worker receives a full wage equal to the competitive level and the employer makes no profit. The worker's daily pay is HA; the worker's wage rate is reflected by the slope of the ray from the origin to point A (here shown by the dashed line OA).[16] Note that if the employer pays this wage for each hour of work, he will have to limit the worker's hours of work to H, since the worker would prefer to work still more hours at this wage rate.

The effect of a minimum wage is shown in figure 8. A minimum wage will require the employer to pay a daily wage on a ray from the origin that has a steeper slope than OA; in figure 8, this is shown by ray OB. The worker's daily income must be on OB.

We will now examine the effect of minimum wages using the same two extreme cases used for effort and fringe benefits. In the first extreme case, where the supply of labor force participation to the covered sector is perfectly inelastic, employers can lower full wages until they suffer no loss in profits. In this case, employers will cut back their hours of work to H_1, paying their workers H_1C per day and not suffering any losses. Workers are worse off because their utility curve going through C (not shown) is at a level of utility

---

[16] The slope of a schedule is the "rise over the run." The worker's average hourly wage is his daily income (HA) divided by his hours of work (OH); that is, his hourly wage is the slope of OA, the "rise" (HA) over the "run" (OH). (Note that, for expository purposes, the effect of the overtime law is not considered and the existence of other nonwage aspects of work is ignored.)

56

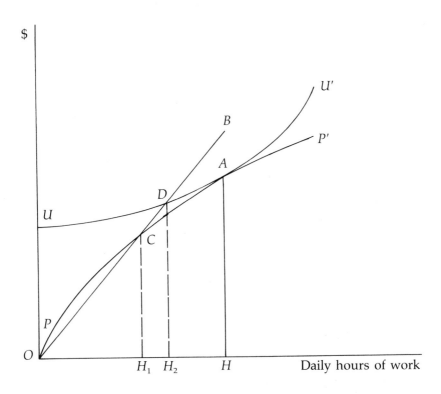

FIGURE 8

MINIMUM WAGES AND HOURS OF WORK WHEN HOURLY
PRODUCTIVITY VARIES BY HOURS WORKED

southeast of UU'. In this case, the daily hours of work will be reduced, but employment will not decline. All workers will be worse off. In the second extreme case, employers cannot reduce the full wage of workers, so that their daily income must be on UU'. The lowest cost point consistent with this restriction and the minimum-wage restraint requiring daily wages to be on ray OB occurs at point D. Obviously the daily productivity of workers at the corresponding hours of work H_2 falls short of the workers' daily cost. Employers will cut back on employment as a result, the cutbacks raising PP' until it intersects point D. In this case, both daily hours of work and employment are reduced, but the worker's full wage remains unchanged. In the intermediary cases, the daily hours of work will be reduced (falling between H_1 and H_2), employment will decline, and workers will have a reduced full wage.

We will now analyze the case where employers react to a min-

FIGURE 9
MINIMUM WAGES AND HOURS OF WORK WHEN DAILY FIXED COST
EXISTS

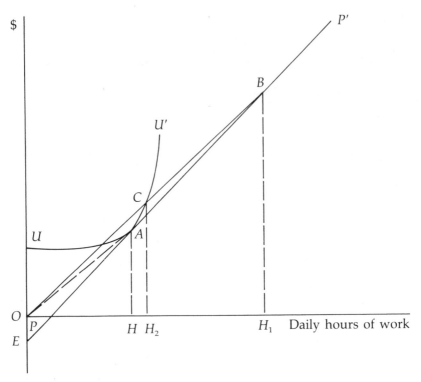

imum-wage increase by increasing their workers' hours of work. Once again we will analyze the case for daily hours of work. The employers that react this way are assumed to have a daily fixed cost for having a worker work each day. In figure 9 this fixed cost is represented by *OE*. *PP'* shows the worker's daily productivity net of this fixed cost. The long-run competitive equilibrium occurs at *H* hours, with the worker on net producing and being paid *HA* a day and an hourly wage represented by the slope of the ray *OA*. *UU'* once again is the worker's utility curve that corresponds to the full wage existing in the absence of a minimum wage.

The presence of a minimum wage increases the slope of the ray on which the employers must have their daily wage payments; this is shown in figure 9 by ray *OB*. In the first extreme case, where employers can make whatever offsets they need to defray any cost of the minimum wage, they will increase their workers' hours of work to H_1. The hourly differential between what the worker is producing and what he is being paid, which initially existed to cover the fixed daily cost, allows the firm to increase its hours of work and use this differential to cover the minimum-wage cost. The worker will be worse off, being on a utility curve lower than UU'. In the second extreme case, the employer must maintain the same full wage, keeping the worker on his utility curve UU' as well as on ray OB. The lowest cost point where these two restraints can be satisfied is point C, with H_2 hours. At H_2 the worker's productivity does not cover his costs, so that the employer will have to cut back on employment until PP' passes through point C. For any intermediary case, the hours of work will fall between H_1 and H_2, with employment and full wages reduced.

In neither of these cases, where employers reduce or increase the hours of work, did we consider the effects of the industrywide changed man-hours on the price of output and thus on the value of the daily productivity of workers. These diagrams assumed that the demand for the output of these employers is perfectly elastic, so that the price does not change. The effect of a less than perfectly elastic demand schedule will be that price, and hence the value of the worker's daily output, will change in the direction opposite to the change in man-hours. The higher price resulting in the first case, when employers reduced their daily hours of work, will keep the employers from reducing the daily hours of workers as much as they would have otherwise, so that the worker's full wage will be decreased less. The lower price resulting in the second case, when employers increase their workers' daily hours of work, will cause the employers to increase the daily hours of work even more, so that the workers' full wage will be decreased more. It is of interest to note that in this second case a minimum-wage increase could result in a lower price of output, especially in the first extreme case, where the labor supply to the covered sector is perfectly inelastic. The same result is possible when employers react to a minimum-wage increase by requiring their workers to expend more effort. For the effort and hours-of-work offsets, then, it is uncertain how the minimum wage will affect the price and output of the affected industries, while for the fringe-benefit offsets, output will be reduced and prices increased to offset the higher minimum-wage costs.

The Expanded Model: A Graphic Presentation

Some of the main forms of offsets have been examined. Employers can react to a minimum-wage increase by reducing fringe benefits, increasing their workers' effort, or changing their workers' hours of work. In general, these offsets are not perfect substitutes to the workers for their increased money wages, so that workers value their losses more than their gains from minimum-wage increases. Alternatively stated, if employers tried to keep their workers' full wage at its preincrease level, they could not fully offset their higher wage costs because of the increase in minimum wages. Employers would then reduce their work force, forcing their disemployed workers into the uncovered sector or out of the labor force, with a result of decreased search income and full wages in the uncovered jobs. The lowered search income would allow covered employers to make even more offsets, lowering the full wages of covered workers. All workers in the economy would have lower full wages, and employment and total labor force participation would be reduced.

The minimum wage in effect acts as a tax on the full wage of workers, creating a wedge between the expenditures the employers are making on their workers and the utility workers derive from these expenditures. Although some of its effects differ, a minimum wage has the same general effects that a tax imposed directly on covered workers would have.

Figure 10 illustrates the two-sector expanded model. The basic schedules shown are similar to those in figure 1, except that the presence of fringe benefits must now be considered. For example, NN' is still the demand schedule of covered employers for labor, but it shows the relationship between the employers' cost per worker (including fringe-benefit costs in addition to wages) and total covered employment. In the absence of a minimum wage, it also shows the full wage that employers can pay workers, given their level of employment. This result follows from the definition of full wages, which treats an additional dollar in money wages as an additional dollar in full wages (ignoring taxes). Because cost-minimizing employers will distribute their expenditures between wages and fringe benefits so that the marginal dollar spent on each yields the same increment to the workers' full wage, it follows that the marginal dollar spent on fringe benefits increases full wages by a dollar. As full wages are measured in the value of the marginal dollars spent on wages and fringe benefits, it follows that in the absence of minimum wages, the employers' expenditures on workers equal their workers' full wage. $N_u N_u'$, similarly, is the demand schedule of employers in the uncovered sector for workers, when measured from the labor force participation schedule, LL'. It shows the relationship that the costs per worker *and* the full wage per worker bear to the level of uncovered employment. From left to right, $N_u N_u'$ is the supply schedule of labor force participants to the covered sector.

FIGURE 10
THE EXPANDED MODEL

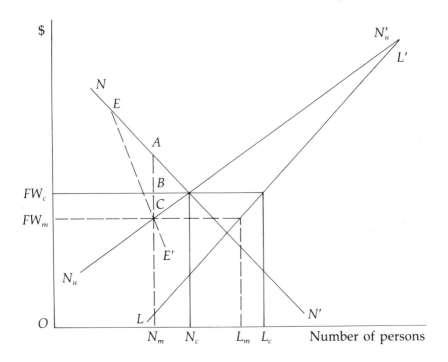

In the absence of a minimum wage, the demand for and supply of workers in each sector will be in equilibrium at the competitive full wage, FW_c. N_c workers will be employed in the covered sector, N_cL_c employed in the uncovered sector, and the size of the labor force will equal L_c.

The introduction of a minimum wage causes employers to make the various offsets described above, so that for a given level of expenditures on their workers, the full wage of their workers will be less. Assume that at point E the wage that employers would be willing to pay equals the minimum wage, so that there will be no offsets when employment is at or to the left of E. To the left of E, then, on NN', the workers' full wage still equals the expenditures being made on them. To the right of E, however, employers, in the absence of a minimum wage, would normally pay lower money wages.[17] The effect of the minimum wage is to force employers to

---

[17] Unless money wages are inferior goods (and they definitely are not), then when the employer's expenditures per worker decrease, he will also reduce wages (if he can).

raise money wages and reduce fringe benefits (as well as to make the other offsets described), lowering the workers' full wage below the expenditures being made on them. The schedule of lowered full wages is shown by EE', the vertical difference between EE' and NN' being the implicit tax due to the minimum wage. EE' is now the demand schedule for covered labor force participants. The new equilibrium level of full wages is FW_m, this being paid to both covered and uncovered workers. N_1 workers are employed in the covered sector, N_1L_1 in the uncovered sector, and labor force participation equals L_1.

In the covered sector, the worker produces AN_m, and the employer is spending the same amount on him. His full wage is only FW_m (or CN_m), however, and the distance AC represents the net cost of the minimum-wage increase. In the case shown, AB is the employers' share of this cost, while BC is the workers' share. By the simple manipulation of the N_uN_u' schedule, the results of the two extreme cases discussed for each offset can be derived. In the first extreme case, with N_uN_u' vertical, the worker will bear the full cost, but employment will not be decreased. In the second extreme case, with N_uN_u' horizontal, the employer will bear the full cost, and employment will be reduced by its maximum extent (at least for the expanded model).

The appendix presents a formal derivation of the expanded model and of the results described in this chapter. In the expanded model, to recapitulate, labor force participation is predicted to decline, along with the full wage of all workers. The price of output may fall or rise, but if it does rise, the increase will be smaller than that predicted by the standard model. These predictions stand in contrast to those of the standard model and will be examined in the next chapter.

The Standard and Expanded Models Combined

In the expanded model, it was assumed that employers made enough offsets so that their workers' full wage was reduced to the level of their search income. There may be several restraints that prevent employers from making this many offsets, however. Three of these restraints are discussed below, and then the effect of those restraints is described.

One restraint is the fixed costs that may be involved in making an offset. When the present value of the offset to the employer is smaller than a fixed cost, the employer will prefer not to make the offset. This consideration is particularly relevant because it suggests that larger and longer-lasting minimum-wage increases will have more negative effects. In the past, inflation and technological advances have served to shorten the period that minimum wages have restrained wages. If minimum wages are indexed to manufacturing wages, however, as has recently been proposed, the effective period of the minimum wage will be considerably longer than for past increases. As a consequence, employers would have a greater incentive to make more offsets if the minimum wage were indexed, with a greater negative effect. Another implication of this consideration is that larger employers may be able to spread the fixed cost of an offset over more workers, so that they will be more likely to make an offset. In this case, workers in large firms may be more harmed by a minimum-wage increase.

A second restraint is that the amount of offsets possible may be less than necessary to reduce full wages to search income. At some point it may be that fringe-benefit expenditures are reduced to zero, all useful effort has been extracted from workers and the hours of work have been adjusted as much as is productively useful. Beyond this point, no further offsets will be possible.

A third restraint is that some of the offsets may be public goods, in that their reduction harms other workers whose wages were above the minimum wage. Examples include air conditioning and the work pace. Employers will have to compensate these other workers for the negative effect of these offsets; if the total of these compensations is too high, the employer may prefer to not make the offsets. An implication is that minimum-wage workers are more likely to be harmed by a minimum-wage increase, the higher the percentage of their fellow workers who are also minimum-wage workers.

As long as these restraints are not effective, the effects of a minimum-wage increase will be explained by the expanded model. Thereafter, however, the standard model must be used. We will focus on the second restraint and suppose that at some point all offsets are exhausted. Figure 11 shows how the effects of a minimum-wage increase could then be analyzed. EE' shows the expanded model's full wage schedule. At FW_m, employers have made all the offsets they can and choose to employ no more workers. From this employment level, N_1, SS' shows the search income schedule of the standard model. The equilibrium search income is S_m, and the full wage in the uncovered sector also equals S_m. In figure 11, the minimum wage reduced covered employment from N_c to N_m, causing N_mN_2 workers to remain unemployed and searching for jobs in the covered sector and leaving N_2L_m workers in the uncovered sector. In the case shown, the minimum wage has benefited all workers;

FIGURE 11
THE TWO MODELS COMBINED

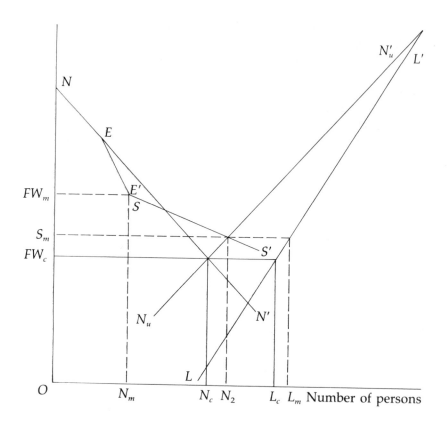

it is equally possible to show a case where all workers, or just employed workers who are not covered, are worse off.

From this analysis and, in particular, from the consideration of the second restraint (that is, the offsets that can be made are limited), one can derive the implication that the standard model's result will apply to a greater extent when the amount of fringe benefits (and other offsets) is small relative to the size of the minimum increase. Unfortunately, there is little information upon which to judge the possible extent to which offsets can be made. An ad hoc conjecture is that young workers, particularly teen-age females, may have less attachment to the work force on average and thus may have a smaller demand for fringe benefits. For example, they may have a smaller demand for on-the-job training and pensions. If this is the case, their employers' offsets, at least for fringe benefits, will be smaller, and the standard model will be relatively more important for them. Even if the standard model's results do apply, however, the expanded model presented here shows that even when minimum-wage increases have increased the full wage of covered workers, the increase is smaller than previously thought.

4

The Effects of Minimum Wages:
An Empirical Analysis

The predictions of the standard and expanded models will be examined in this chapter to determine which is more appropriate for describing the effects of minimum wages. According to the standard model, a minimum-wage increase will raise prices and costs significantly, reduce the quit rate of covered workers, and increase labor force participation (in most cases). According to the expanded model, it will have an uncertain effect on prices and on quits and will decrease labor force participation.

The most important variables with which to test the expanded model are the labor force participation rate and the quit rate. By looking at what workers do—by examining their choice to enter the job search and their choice to leave their jobs—it is possible to determine how minimum wages have affected the full wage of the job. It might be asserted, in contrast, that it is more important to look at the effects of minimum wages on specific fringe benefits (as we did in chapter 1). In fact, however, these observations on offsets would be inconclusive. If, for example, the minimum-wage increase did not reduce specific fringe benefits, nothing would be proved because other less easily measured offsets could have been made. And if a minimum-wage increase did reduce several fringe benefits, we would still be unable to say how much these offsets affected workers or whether their full wage was, on net, increased or decreased. Only by looking at what workers do—only by looking at labor force participation and quit rates—can welfare judgments be made about the effects of minimum wages on the full wages of the covered jobs.

Another important variable with which to test the expanded model is the price of the output produced by covered employers. A measure of the extent of offsets that employers make is the degree to which prices do not increase in response to a minimum-wage increase. We will now examine how minimum wages have affected prices.

The Impact of Minimum Wages on Prices

Ideally we would like to measure the effects of a minimum wage on the cost of each unit of output as a way of establishing the extent to which employers were able to offset its impact on wage costs. These offsets include not only those described in chapter 1 (such as reducing fringe benefits and increasing worker effort) but also such conventional offsets as reducing output, shifting technology, and substituting capital for labor. The empirical evidence from many industrial studies suggests that these conventional offsets are not substantial, at least for the short periods of time of adjustment that we will be studying. Thus the main offsets being made to keep costs down will be those described in chapter 1, although the presence of the conventional offsets cannot be ignored.

When employers sell their output in competitive markets, the price of their output will correspond to their marginal cost of producing each unit of output. Most evidence suggests that these employers are in competitive markets; so we will treat the price of output as an equivalent measure of the effects of minimum wages on costs.

The Bureau of Labor Statistics has published several studies on the prices of covered industries before and after an increase in the minimum wage.[1] The prices of goods produced by southern industries were contrasted with the prices of similar goods produced outside the South (the "non-South"). We will use these data to examine the effects of minimum wages on the prices of southern goods relative to nonsouthern goods. By examining the change in relative prices, we can remove the effect of those factors that are common to all regions of the nation, such as inflation. If the remaining factors are randomly distributed between regions, the change in relative prices will serve as a statistically valid measure of the impact of minimum wages on costs.

As the wage costs of southern firms are more severely increased by minimum wages than those of nonsouthern firms, the standard

---

[1] The effect of minimum wages on prices is presented in U.S. Department of Labor, Wage and Hour and Public Contract Division, *An Evaluation of the Minimum Wage and Maximum Hour Standards of the Fair Labor Standards Act*, Washington, D.C., 1965, table 35, and *Minimum Wages and Maximum Hours Standards under the Fair Labor Standards Act*, Washington, D.C., August 1969, table 12.

model predicts that a minimum-wage hike should increase the relative prices of southern goods produced by covered firms. For example, the 1967 increase in the minimum wage increased the wage costs of the southern hotel and motel industry by 7.3 percent but increased wage costs only 2 percent nationally. For eating and drinking establishments, the same figures were 3.2 percent and 0.7 percent, respectively. If there are no offsets, the relative prices of southern goods should be increased by the difference in the percentage by which wage costs are increased in southern and nonsouthern firms, multiplied by the share of labor costs in total costs. If labor represents half the total cost of producing output, the minimum-wage increase should have increased the relative prices of southern goods by between 2 and 3 percent.

A limitation of using relative prices is that in a competitive market the price of identical goods should be equal. As a result, if southern and nonsouthern industries sell their goods in the same markets and if consumers regard these goods as nearly the same, then a minimum wage will have no effect on the relative prices of southern goods, even in the standard model. For this result to occur, however, a corollary result is that southern employment should be relatively reduced by the minimum wage increase. There is some evidence that this does occur,[2] but the evidence is weak, and the suggested relative reduction in employment for the short span of time we will be studying seems to be small. It appears, then, that southern firms can pass a substantial proportion of their higher relative costs on to consumers in the form of higher prices. Nevertheless, this limitation weakens the use of price data as a tool to contrast the expanded and standard models.

Table 4 presents the effects of minimum wages on the relative price of southern industries covered by the minimum-wage law. The first half of the table shows the effects of the 1961 increase of 15 percent, and the second half shows the 1967 increase of 12 percent. Of the goods surveyed, 45 percent had a reduction in their relative price. Only two of the industries surveyed, lumber and services, had a significant increase in their relative price, these increases being within the range suggested by the standard model. For the other industries, however, the minimum wage had no significant impact on relative prices. Overall, the ambiguous effect of minimum wages

---

[2] The reduction of southern employment by minimum wages is analyzed in David E. Kaun, "Economics of the Minimum Wage: The Effects of the Fair Labor Standards Act, 1945–60" (Ph.D. diss., Stanford University, 1963). His results are discussed in John M. Peterson and Charles T. Stewart, Jr., *Employment Effects of Minimum Wage Rates* (Washington, D.C.: American Enterprise Institute, 1969), pp. 44–50.

TABLE 4

Relative Change in Prices, South versus Non-South, for Selected Industries

Group	Number with Relative Price Increase	Average[a] Price Increase(%)	Number with Relative Price Decrease	Average Price Decrease	Average Relative Price Change for Industry, % (t-statistic)
	Relative change in prices, August 1961–August 1962[b]				
Textiles industry	10	1.60	6	−2.40%	0.0 (0.0)
Lumber and wood products industry	4	2.41	0	—	2.41 (1.7)
Furniture industry	9	1.71	4	−3.31	0.14 (0.2)
	Relative change in prices, 1966–1967[c]				
Industry	9	1.36	6	−4.72	−1.08 (−.9)
Services	6	2.80	1	−0.10	2.71 (2.7)

NOTE: The change in prices reported here is the percentage change in the relative prices of southern over nonsouthern goods (i.e., approximately the percentage change in southern prices minus the percentage change in nonsouthern prices).
[a] The averages in these tabulations are unweighted summations of the percentage changes in prices of the various goods reported by the Bureau of Labor Statistics.
[b] For minimum-wage increase, September 1961.
[c] For minimum-wage increase, February 1967 (October–October for industry, September–September for service).

on relative prices shown in table 4 is more consistent with the expanded model. In the expanded model, prices can be increased or decreased, and any increase will be smaller than that predicted by the standard model. Nevertheless, the standard model (in light of the limitations noted) could be consistent with these data, so that, by itself, this evidence is insufficient to distinguish between the two models.

The Impact of Minimum Wages on Quit Rates

A worker will quit his job when its full wage falls short of his search income. Although an employer may not know the full wage and search income of each of his workers, he will undoubtedly be aware to some degree of the relationship between his expenditures on his workers and their corresponding quit rate. As he spends more, the full wage of his average worker should be increased relative to search income, resulting in a lower quit rate. We will treat employers in this section as if they knew their average worker's full wage and search income, so that employers choose their quit rate by their choice of full wages.

In the standard model, employers do not make any offsets; a minimum-wage increase is thus predicted by the standard model to increase their full wages relative to search income, so that their quit rate will be reduced. In the expanded model, on the other hand, employers can select the full wages that they pay by making the necessary number of offsets. The effect of minimum wages on the quit rate in the expanded model thus depends on the choices of employers.[3] There is likely to be a difference between their short-run and long-run choices of quit rates; we now examine their choice of short-term quit rates.

Immediately after a minimum-wage increase, covered employers, even in the expanded model, will want to reduce their work force.[4] They may choose to do this through an increased quit rate by reducing their workers' full wages relative to search income. This reduction in the differential between full wages and search income (of the average worker) would be temporary, persisting only long enough for the work force to reach its lower desired size. Other methods that may be used in place of or with an increased quit rate are reduced hires and increased layoffs. For example, in past recessions the quit rate has typically fallen, indicating that employers prefer the alternative methods of reducing their work force. In any case, it is a possible but not necessary outcome of the expanded model that a minimum-wage increase will cause a temporary increase in the quit rate. An alternative to this disemployment explanation of an increased quit rate is the possibility that covered workers take time to learn the value of their potential search income. After a minimum-wage increase, when employers lower the full wage of

---

[3] The interaction between employers and workers in the determination of quit rates is discussed in Walter J. Wessels, "The Contribution by Firms to Unemployment: A Dynamic Model," *Southern Economic Journal,* vol. 45, no. 4 (April 1979), pp. 1130–50.
[4] In our empirical work, we will assume that firms adjust to minimum wages after a hike. On the other hand, an increase in the minimum wage that is anticipated will cause employers to adjust the size of their work force before the actual increase if there are fixed costs to hiring and firing workers and if these costs increase more than proportionately when the turnover rate is increased. The earlier adjustment would allow firms to even out and lower their overall costs.

their workers, some of the workers may quit, not realizing that their search income has been reduced by the minimum wage. As in the case described, this increased quit rate will be transitory, returning to its normal level when workers adjust their perceived search income to its actual level.

To study the temporary effect of minimum wages on quit rates, we used a method similar to that used by Parsons in his study of turnover rates.[5] The quit rates of various low-wage covered industries identified by the Bureau of Labor Statistics as being seriously affected by minimum wages were studied.

The log of the quit rate for each industry was regressed on the log of the hourly wages for production workers in manufacturing establishments, the log of the hourly wages in the industry, the log of the vacancy rate, and a minimum-wage variable. The hourly wages of production workers and the industry's own wages serve to control for the main factors influencing the differential between full wages and search income. The vacancy rate reflects the availability of jobs and also affects search income. The minimum-wage variable was the percentage change in the minimum wage; the change in this variable—first increasing and then decreasing—captures the predicted short-run changes in the quit rate. In addition, two time-trend variables and a set of monthly dummy variables were included to control for long-term and seasonal factors. One variable that Parsons had used but omitted in these regressions was the level of industrial output. One reason for this omission was that the variable was not available for all the industries studied. Another reason was that output is likely to be affected endogenously by the minimum wage; the same is true of the industry's own wage, but a set of regressions omitting this variable did not alter the estimated effect of minimum wages significantly in almost every case.

The results of these regressions are shown in table 5. The 1966 annual average hourly wage is shown for each industry listed (in 1966 the minimum wage was $1.25). The industries are listed according to the level of their wages, the lower-wage industries being listed first. Presumably, the lower-wage industries should be more seriously affected by the minimum wage. The next column shows the short-run response of quit rates to the short-run minimum-wage variable described (the percentage change in the minimum wage). The last column shows the response of the quit rate to the level of minimum wages.

---

[5] Donald O. Parsons, "Quit Rates over Time: A Search and Information Approach," *American Economic Review*, vol. 63, no. 3 (June 1973), pp. 390–401.

TABLE 5

Effect of Minimum Wages on Quit Rates

Industry and SIC code	1966 Wage	Effect of Minimum Wage on Quits, %[a] (t-statistic)	
		Short-run	Long-run
Men's and boys' furnishings (232)	1.59	0.48 (.46)	0.59 (1.60)[b]
Hosiery, not elsewhere classified (2252)	1.62	−0.72 (−.41)	0.88 (1.07)
Women's and children's undergarments (234)	1.67	1.01 (1.04)	0.35 (1.01)
Cigars (212)	1.77	−1.32 (−.73)	−1.06 (−1.42)[b]
Wooden containers (244)	1.82	1.03 (.58)	−0.02 (−.02)
Yarn and thread mills (228)	1.83	−0.65 (−.58)	−0.42 (−1.00)
Knitting mills (225)	1.85	−0.63 (−.67)	−0.04 (−.12)
Footwear, except rubber (314)	1.87	0.22 (.26)	−0.82 (−3.02)[b]
Narrow fabric mills (224)	1.92	0.81 (.55)	0.24 (.48)
Weaving mills, cotton (221)	1.98	0.76 (.87)	0.16 (.40)
Toys and sporting goods (394)	2.01	1.56 (1.28)	−0.58 (−1.59)[b]
Costume jewelry and notions (396)	2.05	−0.47 (−.28)	−0.02 (−.03)
Household furniture (251)	2.08	−0.68 (−.63)	0.10 (.16)
Miscellaneous wood products (249)	2.11	−1.43 (−1.06)	−0.21 (−.33)
Sawmills and planing mills (242)	2.12	−0.05 (−.04)	−1.16 (−1.88)[b]
Confectionery products (2071)	2.13	−0.03 (−.04)	−0.92 (−2.13)[b]
Pens, pencils, office and art supplies (395)	2.15	−1.32 (−.70)	0.17 (.26)
Miscellaneous textile products (229)	2.19	0.99 (1.12)	−0.19 (−.67)
Brick and structural clay tiles (3251)	2.19	1.75 (1.18)	0.61 (1.41)[b]
Confectionery and related products (207)	2.20	0.97 (.64)	0.89 (1.49)[b]
Men's and boys' suits (231)	2.24	0.77 (.69)	−0.80 (−2.35)[b]
Millwork, plywood, related products (243)	2.42	−0.63 (−.51)	0.31 (.66)

TABLE 5 (continued)

Industry and SIC code	1966 Wage	Effect of Minimum Wage on Quits, %[a] (t-statistic)	
		Short-run	Long-run
Leather tanning and furnishings (311)	2.50	3.03 (2.17)[b]	0.29 (.73)
Bakery products (205)	2.59	−0.46 (−.46)	0.53 (1.07)
Cigarettes (211)	2.69	4.39 (1.88)[b]	−1.16 (−1.89)[b]

NOTE: SIC stands for standard industrial classification.

[a] The dependent variable was the natural log of the quit rate of the industry. The independent variables were the log of the hourly wage of workers in that industry, the log of the hourly wage for production workers in manufacturing (excluding overtime), the log of the vacancy rate, a set of monthly dummy variables, and two time-trend variables (one increasing by unity each month, the other being the square of the first). The minimum-wage variable for the short-run column was the percentage change in the minimum wage, while it was the log of the level of the minimum wage in the long-run column. An Alman distributed log with two degrees of freedom and a four-month lag were used for the first three variables as well as for the minimum-wage variable. A Cochrane-Orcutt procedure was used to remove autocorrelation. The data were monthly, from January 1958 through December 1969.

[b] Significant (one-tail) at the 10 percent level.

From the table, it can be seen that no industry had a significant decrease in its quit rate in the short run. On the other hand, two industries had significant increases in their quit rates. These results correspond with those of the expanded model but contradict those of the standard model.

In the long run, after employers have reduced their work force to the desired size and workers have reduced their perceived search income to its actual level, the effect of minimum wages in the expanded model may be to reduce the quit rate. Recall that in the expanded model employers constrained by the minimum wage will reduce their nonwage expenditures, so that an additional dollar spent on a worker (on his fringe benefits or by reducing some other offset) will increase his full wages by more than a dollar. It follows that it is cheaper for such an employer (relative to unconstrained employers) to purchase a greater differential between the full wage and search income of its average worker. With a set of turnover costs similar to those unconstrained employers, these employers will purchase a greater differential and a lower quit rate.[6] The prediction of both the standard and the expanded models for the long-term effects of minimum wages on the quit rate is similar: quit rates should be reduced.

To study the long-run effects of minimum wages on the quit rate, we ran the same regressions with a different minimum-wage variable: we used the log value of the actual level of the minimum wage. These results are presented in the last column of table 5.

In several industries the quit rate was significantly reduced by minimum wages, but in many others it was not significantly changed. This latter result is possible only in the context of the expanded model and is consistent with the case where money wages are a close substitute for the offsets the employers make. It is of interest to note that at a 10 percent level of significance (that is, at only a 10 percent chance of being wrong because of random errors), three of the industries had a significantly positive increase in their quit rate (as opposed to seven that had a significant negative decrease in their quit rate). A possible, but admittedly ad hoc, explanation for a long-run increase in the quit rate is that a minimum-wage increase may

---

[6] To show this, consider the case of a firm whose average cost per worker is $W + B + \gamma T$, where W is its wage cost, B is its fringe benefit cost, γ is its turnover rate, and T is its turnover cost if a worker leaves. The average turnover cost per worker is thus γT. Let γ be a negative function of full wages, FW, which in turn is a positive function of W and B. On the margin, the firm will spend another dollar on fringe benefits if it gains a corresponding dollar reduction in its average turnover costs. Or, at the optimal level of B, we will have

$$1 = -\frac{\partial \gamma}{\partial FW}\frac{\partial FW}{\partial B}T$$

For the unconstrained firm, $\partial FW/\partial B = 1$ on the margin, so that

$$\frac{\partial \gamma}{\partial FW} = -\frac{1}{T}$$

For the firm constrained by the minimum wage, a dollar more spent on fringe benefits increases full wages by even more than a dollar (so that $\partial FW/\partial B = b > 1$), or

$$\frac{\partial \gamma}{\partial FW} = -\frac{1}{bT}$$

If γ decreases at a decreasing rate with higher full wages (as it will near its optimal level), then the full wage (relative to the value of search) must be higher to minimum-wage firms, since the marginal effect of another dollar of fringe benefits on quits must be smaller for it ($bT > T$). See Walter J. Wessels, *The Effects of Minimum Wages on the Youth Labor Market: An Expanded Model*, Technical Analysis Paper no. 66 (Washington, D.C.: U.S. Department of Labor, Office of the Assistant Secretary for Policy, Evaluation, and Research, July 1979), pp. 26–32.

74

reduce the investment by employers in their workers' training, so that employers are less reluctant to have their workers quit.

Although the long-run effects of minimum wages are to reduce the quit rates of several industries, the increased quit rate of some industries in the short run is possible only in the expanded model. There is, however, a possible exception in the standard model, a case where the quit rate of some industries could be increased. Imagine that all workers are equally skilled and, in a competitive labor market, that all jobs initially pay the same full wage. With time, as jobs vary in their nonwage aspects, their money wages will differ, some employers paying a lower money wage than others. A minimum wage will most raise the money wage of the employers previously paying a lower wage, while the money wage of the employers previously paying a higher wage will be only slightly affected. If employers do not make offsets, the full wage of the employers previously paying a lower wage will be higher than the full wage of the other employers; workers in the jobs that previously had a higher wage may then quit to take the jobs with previously lower wages that are now paying a higher full wage. For this to occur, it is necessary that the minimum wage increase search income; the next section indicates that this does *not* occur. It seems even more unlikely because the jobs previously carrying the lower wage will have the greatest reduction in their job openings (at least in the context of the standard model), so that the potential search costs of seeking these jobs will be even higher.

The Effect of Minimum Wages on Labor Force Participation

To determine how a minimum-wage increase affects the welfare of unemployed and uncovered workers (as well as of covered workers in the context of the expanded model), it is necessary to know how it affects the value of search. There are three different ways of measuring how the value of search has been affected. One way is to measure the effect of minimum wages on the wages of uncovered employers, since these wages correspond to the search income of workers.[7] Unfortunately, we do not have data on the wages of un-

[7] George Tauchen, "The Minimum Wage and Job Search" (Ph.D. diss., University of Minnesota, 1978), examined the effects of minimum wages on uncovered agricultural wages as well as on the wages of covered low-wage employers. A central limitation is that both industries employ higher-wage labor whose wage changes may offset the wage changes of low-wage labor. In any case, Tauchen found that the minimum wage did lower uncovered wages nationally and particularly in the South and Southwest, but he found that his measure of uncovered wages was increased in the Northeast and the upper Midwest.

covered employers over any significant period of time. It is therefore necessary to devise a proxy measure of these wages, whose validity as a tool for measuring search income is open to question. A second way is to measure the effect of minimum wages on uncovered employment, which should be negatively related to the change in search income. This measure also suffers from an unavailability of data. A third way, and the way we will use, is to measure the effect of minimum wages on labor force participation. Data on labor force participation are available not only for the whole work force but also for many age, race, and sex cohorts of the population, allowing for a detailed analysis of how minimum wages affect the search income of various segments of our society. One disadvantage is that, unlike the first measure of uncovered wages, the changes in labor force participation tell us only whether search income has been increased or decreased, but not by how much. To know how much, we need to know how responsive each group's labor force participation is to changes in search income, something we do not know for all cohorts.

The use of labor force participation is predicated on the assumption that it is positively correlated with search income, so that it increases when search income increases. The only possible case where this will not occur is when a minimum wage increases nonwork income more than search income. To illustrate how this might occur, suppose a minimum wage raises the full income and search income of all workers. A single unattached worker would then never leave the work force, since the minimum wage leaves his nonwork income unaffected (although it could cause him to want to work fewer hours). Still, a worker in a family may have an increased nonwork income because some of the other family members now earn more, lessening his (or her) need to work and thereby increasing his nonwork income. If this increase in nonwork income is large enough, this worker may drop out of the labor force. A central question is, How strong is this indirect effect? The evidence suggests that it is weak, so that an increase in the value of search will lead to an increase, not a decrease, in labor force participation. A main reason that this indirect effect is likely to be weak is that the actual impact of minimum wages on family income has been small. Kelly, for example, measured the reduction in the poverty gap (the difference between the government's definition of poverty income and actual family income) when all working family members earn (at a minimum) various hypothetical levels of the minimum wage.[8] This

---

[8] Terence F. Kelly, *Two Policy Questions regarding the Minimum Wage*, Working Paper 3608–05 (Washington, D.C.: Urban Institute, 1976).

reduction will be overstated, since some family members could be disemployed by the minimum wage and others may be in uncovered jobs.

Despite this overstatement, the calculated reductions in the gap were small. For example, if the minimum wage had been $2.50 an hour (at a time when it was increased from $1.60 to $2.00), the poverty gap would have been reduced by only 5.1 percent. A minimum wage of $3.50 would have reduced it by only 9.2 percent. The resulting increases in family income would have been even smaller than these percentages. It appears, then, that many of those affected by minimum wages are not in poor families, so that minimum wages have little effect on family income. Confirming this result, Gramlich found that of the low-wage workers (who earned $2.00 an hour or less in 1973, when the minimum wage was $1.60), almost one-third were members of families whose income exceeded the median income in the United States.[9] Thus the increase in family income resulting from minimum-wage increases appears to be small; but even if it were sizable, various econometric studies show that one family member's nonwork income is not substantially affected by the other family members' income.[10] From these studies, it appears that the indirect effect of minimum wages on nonwork income is weak, so that its direct impact on the value of search will predominate and search income and labor force participation will change together in the same direction.

Because in the past the prime emphasis has been on the effects of minimum wages on employment and unemployment, there have been relatively few studies of its effects on labor force participation. We will review three of the main studies here. The first is that of Kaitz, who introduced a minimum-wage variable that expressed the minimum wage as a proportion of the average hourly earnings weighted by industry teen-age employment and minimum-wage coverage.[11] He studied effects of minimum wages on teen-age labor

---

[9] Edward M. Gramlich, *Impact of Minimum Wages on Other Wages, Employment, and Family Income*, Brookings Papers on Economic Activity, no. 2 (Washington, D.C.: Brookings Institution, 1976).

[10] James Heckman, "The Common Structure of Statistical Models of Truncation, Sample Selection and Limited Dependent Variables and a Simple Estimator for Such Models," *Annals of Economic and Social Measurement*, vol. 5, no. 4 (Fall 1976), pp. 475–92, and Geraldo Barros, "Asking Wages, Market Wages, and the Off-Farm Labor Supply by Farm Operators" (Ph.D. diss., North Carolina State University, 1976), found very low elasticities (less than 0.2) between the wages or earnings of some household members and the nonwork reservation wage of other household members.

[11] Hyman B. Kaitz, "Experience of the Past: The National Minimum," in *Youth Unemployment and Minimum Wages*, Bureau of Labor Statistics Bulletin 1657 (Washington, D.C.: U.S. Department of Labor, 1970), pp. 30–54.

force participation and found that its effects were negative for most teen-age cohorts. The only cohorts for whom labor force participation was increased were nonwhite females (sixteen to seventeen and eighteen to nineteen years old) and nonwhite males (eighteen to nineteen). Unfortunately, his study did not report the necessary statistics to determine whether these results could have been due to random error or whether they were significant. I ran a similar set of regressions over the same cohorts and found that only white female teen-agers (sixteen to seventeen and eighteen to nineteen) were significantly affected, their labor force participation being reduced by the minimum wage. The second main study is that of Mincer.[12] To evaluate his results, it is first necessary to discuss the benefits and costs of partitioning the population into cohorts and examining each cohort separately. The benefit of finer partitioning of the population into smaller cohorts is that the individual behavior of each cohort is more easily discernible. The cost of a finer partitioning is that, at least for labor force statistics, there is a smaller sample size, with smaller cohorts and hence a greater possibility for sampling errors.[13] For the nonwhite cohorts that Kaitz looked at, for example, the variation in labor force participation from month to month is unbelievably large. The gain of combining several cohorts is that the relative size of sampling error is reduced, but the cost is inability to detect differences in the individual behavior of the smaller cohorts.

Mincer partitioned the teen-age population less finely than Kaitz, combining sixteen- to seventeen-year-olds with eighteen- to nineteen-year-olds and male with female teen-agers. He found that the minimum wage significantly reduced the labor force participation of white and nonwhite teen-agers. He also found that minimum wages had reduced the labor force participation rate of white males twenty to twenty-four, nonwhite males twenty to twenty-four, white males over sixty-five, and females over twenty. No cohort he studied had a significant increase in labor force participation. The third main study is that of Ragan.[14] He studied cohorts even more finely partitioned than Kaitz's, using enrollment in school as a partitioning criterion as well as age (sixteen to seventeen and eighteen to nine-

---

[12] Jacob Mincer, "Unemployment Effects of Minimum Wages," *Journal of Political Economy*, vol. 84, no. 4, pt. 2 (August 1976), supplement, pp. 87–104.
[13] According to Finis Welch, "Minimum Wage Legislation in the United States," *Economic Inquiry*, vol. 12, no. 3 (September 1974), pp. 285–318, the statistics collected by the Bureau of Labor Statistics contained sizable sampling errors for certain teen-age cohorts (see p. 295).
[14] James F. Ragan, Jr., "Minimum Wages and the Youth Labor Market," *Review of Economics and Statistics*, vol. 54, no. 2 (May 1977), pp. 129–36.

teen), sex (male and female), and race (white and nonwhite). Not surprisingly, then, he found only two cohorts whose labor force participation was significantly affected by the minimum wage; one consisted of nonwhite males enrolled in school and sixteen to seventeen years old, whose labor force participation was reduced, and the other was nonenrolled white females sixteen to seventeen, whose labor force participation was increased.

To study minimum wages further, I examined their effects on several groups in the population. The groups were primarily low-wage groups, since most workers, particularly male adult workers, are hardly affected by minimum wages at all. This consideration leads to one central limitation in all minimum-wage studies, including this one. The limitation is that we have data only on large groups of workers, of whom only a small proportion are directly affected by minimum wages. Even though the minimum-wage law covers most workers, only a small fraction have wages low enough to be directly affected by the minimum wage, which is substantially below the wages of most workers; and evidently, even of those low-wage covered workers, approximately 30 percent illegally receive a wage below the minimum; that is, their employers do not comply with the law.[15]

To take account of the limitation that not all workers are covered by the minimum wage, the studies described used the minimum-wage variable developed by Kaitz, which expressed the minimum wage as a fraction of industrial wages, weighting each industry by its covered employment. As long as the limitation described above—that not all covered workers are affected by the minimum wage—does not change in its relative effectiveness over time, the use of the Kaitz-like minimum wage will accurately measure the proportionate (but not absolute) effect of minimum wages.

Table 6 presents the estimated effect of minimum wages on various groups' labor force participation, using a Kaitz-like minimum-wage variable. The equations fitted to the data are similar to those of Mincer. Other forms were also tested (including those using the variables employed by Kaitz), but these results are not shown, since the minimum wage generally had a statistically similar effect for all forms tested. The form of the equations fitted is described in the footnote to table 6.

The results given in table 6 show that, corresponding to the prediction of the expanded model, minimum wages reduced (or left

---

[15] Orley Ashenfelter and Robert S. Smith, "Compliance with the Minimum Wage Law," *Journal of Political Economy*, vol. 87, no. 2 (April 1979), pp. 333–50.

TABLE 6

THE ELASTICITY OF LABOR FORCE PARTICIPATION WITH RESPECT TO A MINIMUM-WAGE (KAITZ-LIKE) VARIABLE

Worker	Minimum Wage (t-statistic)
Male	
Teen-agers	
16–17	−0.0957 (−1.02)
18–19	−0.1528 (−3.68)[a]
White 16–19	−0.1256 (−1.88)[b]
Nonwhite 16–19	−0.1768 (−1.84)[b]
Young adults	
20–24	−0.0405 (−1.99)[a]
Older adults	
55–64	0.0214 (1.37)
65 and older	0.1743 (2.08)[a]
Female	
Teen-agers	
16–17	−0.0591 (−.51)
18–19	−0.0458 (−.67)
White 16–19	−0.1548 (−1.65)[b]
Nonwhite 16–19	−0.0661 (−.50)
Young adults	
20–24	0.0745 (2.07)[a]
Older adults	
55–64	0.0388 (1.16)
65 and older	−0.0300 (−.33)

NOTE: The independent variables were a constant term, male adult unemployment (ages 35–55), fraction of group in adult (16+) population, fraction in armed forces (for male teen-age and young adult groups only), two time-trend variables (time and time-squared), seasonal dummies, and a Kaitz-like minimum-wage variable (supplied to me by Terence Kelly). The first three variables as well as the minimum-wage variable were entered in log form. The dependent variable was the log of the group's labor force participation rate. The minimum-wage variable was lagged with a two-degree polynomial distributed log for four periods. A Cochrane-Orcutt procedure was adjusted for autocorrelation in the error term. The results of these equations are available from the author on request. Data are quarterly, from 1954 through 1974.
[a] Significant at the 5 percent level.
[b] Significant at the 10 percent level.

unaffected) labor force participation. Teen-age and young adult male workers, in particular, who make up a large fraction of those affected by minimum wages, were negatively affected by the minimum wage. Contrary to the predictions of the expanded model, the labor force participation of young adult females and older males over age sixty-five was significantly increased by the minimum wage. This contrary result may be due to the demand of these groups for relatively fewer fringe benefits, so that the standard model's results are more applicable to them. Alternatively, employers may substitute more highly skilled, higher-wage workers for minimum-wage workers, because the former, after a minimum-wage increase, will have a lower cost per unit of output. If these workers with the higher wage were relatively more numerous in the young female and older male groups, the positive substitution effect on such workers may have been stronger than the negative effect of the expanded model on the minimum-wage workers. Further testing will be needed to determine which of these two alternatives, if either, is more applicable. Also of note in table 6 is the smaller negative effect of minimum wages on females (relative to males) and on teen-age males ages sixteen and seventeen (relative to older teen-age and young adult males).[16] This result corresponds to the ad hoc conjecture that younger teen-agers and females will demand relatively fewer fringe benefits and hence will be more positively affected by minimum wages. On the other hand, the standard model would suggest that these less-skilled groups would be more negatively affected by the minimum wage, a conjecture that appears to be wrong.

As previously stated, the use of the Kaitz-like minimum-wage variable will yield accurate proportionate results when the number of truly affected workers remains relatively constant in relation to the number of covered workers. In fact, though, the recent extensions of coverage in the minimum wages (resulting from the 1961, 1966, and 1974 amendments) offered them to lower-wage workers,

---

[16] To determine the effect of minimum wages on affected workers, it is necessary to estimate the fraction of affected workers in each cohort and then increase the estimated coefficient of minimum wages by dividing it by this fraction. Thus, if one-half of a cohort was affected, and these by 10 percent, the whole cohort would show only a 5 percent effect. By dividing by one-half, the true effect is estimated. Obviously a smaller fraction of the older groups will be affected, and thus their minimum-wage coefficient should be increased. Using data supplied to me by Paul Flaim from tables tabulated by Vera Pernella (*Young Workers and Their Earnings*, Bureau of Labor Statistics Special Labor Force Report no. 132, U.S. Department of Labor, 1971), I found: of male teen-agers between the ages of sixteen and seventeen, 44 percent earned between $1.30 and $1.74 (when the minimum wage was $1.60 in 1969), while for males eighteen to nineteen years old, the figure was 26 percent. If these percentages correspond to the percentage of affected workers, then the older male group is more harmed by the minimum wage at a significance level of 20 percent (with a t-value of .99). In 1975 the percentage of workers earning between $2.00 and $2.49 (when the minimum wage was $2.10) was 13 percent for males twenty to twenty-four years old and 42 percent for white males sixteen to nineteen. The two groups were harmed the same amount, which, considering that older group probably has a more inelastic supply of labor force participation, is surprising.

such as farm, retail, and domestic workers. As a consequence, the change in coverage corresponding to these extensions will understate the actual change in the number of affected workers. To avoid this potential source of error in the Kaitz-like minimum-wage variable, I fitted equations like those in table 6 except that they used a minimum-wage variable that expressed minimum wages as a fraction of hourly manufacturing wages (exclusive of overtime pay) and a set of dummy variables that corresponded to the major changes in coverage. These results are shown in table 7. The dummy variables for changes in coverage were decidedly insignificant in all groups, except for nonwhite female teen-agers, where the increases in coverage resulted in a significant increase in labor force participation. The effect of minimum wages shown in table 7 is similar to effects shown in table 6. The main difference is that the effect of minimum wages is more significantly negative for white female teen-agers (sixteen to nineteen) and young female teen-agers (sixteen to seventeen) in table 7 than in table 6. The general impact of minimum wages also seems more severe for the less-skilled groups in table 7 than in table 6. In both tables, however, the expanded model's prediction of a negative (or neutral) impact of minimum wages appears to be valid for most groups.

To test two hypotheses suggested in the previous chapters, further equations were fitted to the data. First, the standard model suggested that summer workers should be particularly harmed by minimum wages. To test this possibility, the relative summer labor force participation of teen-agers was examined. Their relative participation was measured by dividing the labor force participation for the summer months (June through August) by the remaining year's labor force participation. Then this variable was entered in a regression with the same variables as table 6 (using third-quarter values and, of course, using no seasonal adjustment). This equation was fitted for white male teen-agers, nonwhite male teen-agers, white female teen-agers, and nonwhite female teen-agers. The results for all groups were that the minimum wage had no significant effect on relative summer labor force participation. A second hypothesis tested, with a similar insignificant result, was the suggestion in chapter 1 that unanticipated minimum-wage increases would have an impact different from that of the increases included in past amendments. To test this hypothesis, an equation identical with that in table 6 was fitted to all groups; to the variables in this equation was added one that equaled the value of the minimum-wage variable for the year after a minimum-wage amendment was passed and put into effect and equaled zero otherwise. The coefficient of this vari-

TABLE 7

The Elasticity of Labor Force Participation with Respect to Relative Minimum Wages

Group	Minimum Wage (t-statistic)
Male	
Teen-agers	
16–17	−0.1841 (−.99)
18–19	−0.1521 (−1.34)
White 16–19	−0.2726 (−2.41)[a]
Nonwhite 16–19	0.0635 (.26)
Young adults	
20–24	−0.0409 (−.77)
Older adults	
55–64	0.0459 (1.54)
65 and older	0.3143 (2.61)[a]
Female	
Teen-agers	
16–17	−0.4838 (−2.04)[a]
18–19	−0.0895 (−.57)
White 16–19	−0.5157 (−3.28)[a]
Nonwhite 16–19	−0.2200 (−.59)
Young adults	
20–24	0.1616 (1.71)[b]
Older adults	
55–64	0.0500 (.64)
65 and older	0.1575 (.72)

NOTE: The regressions in this table used the same variables as in table 6 with the following exceptions. First, the minimum-wage variable was the minimum wage divided by the hourly wage of production workers in manufacturing establishments, exclusive of overtime pay. Second, two coverage dummy variables were included, one equaling unity for the period 1961 (third quarter) to 1966 (fourth quarter), the other equaling unity for 1967 (first quarter) through 1972 (first quarter), and both equaling zero in other quarters. The data ran from 1954 through the first quarter in 1972, being limited by the availability of data on manufacturing wages.
[a] Significant at 5 percent level.
[b] Significant at 10 percent level.

able, it was hoped, would capture any additional effects of the newly legislated increases in the minimum wage. Unfortunately, this variable was insignificant in all cases. It may be concluded that these newly legislated increases were as anticipated as the other increases, that firms did not make any anticipatory changes and offsets, or that

83

this variable was inadequate to capture these effects. Clearly, more work is needed in both of the areas suggested here.

Summary

The overall results presented in this chapter confirm the applicability of the expanded model for explaining the effects of minimum wages. The negative or neutral effects of minimum wages on labor force participation, their small effect on prices, and their positive or neutral effect on quit rates correspond with the predictions of the expanded model and not with those of the standard model. As a consequence, it seems a distinct possibility that some covered workers may actually suffer from a minimum-wage increase, while others are not helped as much as their wage increase suggests. If this is the case for most affected workers, there appears to be little justification for the existence of a minimum wage.

Appendix

The basic results presented in the text will be derived here. We will derive, first, the expression for search income presented in equation (2); next, the inequality presented in equation (8); and finally, the reduced-form equations linking minimum wages to search income for both the standard and the expanded models.

At the base of both the standard and the expanded models is the concept of search income. To derive the basic predictions for the standard model, it is necessary to have a simple yet somewhat realistic expression for search income that links it to unemployment and wages. A simple expression, similar to those in the search literature, will be derived here.

The following symbols will be used:

V: The value of search, the present expected value of all future periods of work and search

S: Search income, where $S = rV$

FW: Full wage, the monetary value a worker places on his job's income, including its money and nonmoney wages

W_o: The worker's leisure income if unemployed and not searching for work

C: The full costs of search, including direct costs and forgone time costs

γ: The separation rate from a job, the probability in a given period that a worker will be fired or will quit his job

p: The probability of getting a job offer that is acceptable in a given period of search

r: The rate of time discounting, or the interest rate

The expression for the value of search (V) will be derived from the following assumptions:

A_1 All job searchers are risk-neutral.

A₂   All job searchers make one search per period in a sequential manner until an acceptable offer is found.

A₃   All job searchers plan to work (or search) for an infinite number of periods.

A₄   The search and job markets are stable in the sense that the parameters of search (W_o, S, and p) are unchanging and the parameters of the job are also unchanging (FW and γ).

Basically, these assumptions act to simplify the expression for the value of search. Assumption A_1 could be modified to assume that workers are risk-averse, but there is no evidence regarding the risk attitudes of youth. Assumption A_2 ignores the fact that workers search with differing intensities, but as long as the distribution of these intensities is stable, there would be no need to modify our model. Assumption A_3 is quite unrealistic, but for young workers the additional precision gained from considering a finite work life borders on infinitesimal. Assumption A_4 ignores certain dynamic aspects of search, but its modification would seriously complicate our model.

An expression for the value of search, V, is as follows.

The income from *one* period of job search is the net income "earned" while searching ($W_o - C$) plus the expected wealth to be gained if a job is found (p times the present expected value of a job, VJ):

$$W_o - C + pVJ$$

VJ, a wealth term, appears because it reflects the present value of all future income to be earned if a job is found and search is terminated; it may be thought of, perhaps, as a "prize" given when the searcher finds and accepts a job. It follows, then, that:

$$V = \frac{pVJ + W_o - S}{p + r} \qquad (9)$$

Result (9) follows from the proposition that the present expected value of a potentially infinite stream of "payments" of X per period that has a probability p of terminating in any given period will be $X/(p + r)$.[1] In this case, each period's payment is $pVJ + W_o - C$, and p is the probability that these payments will be terminated.

The present expected value of a job is derived in a similar manner. The income from one period of working is the full wage of the job (FW) plus the expected wealth of having to search for a new job

---

[1] Each payment of X takes place at the end of a period. The first X takes place with certainty (so that one must make one search to get a job), but further payments of

if the job is terminated (γ times V; if a jobholder loses his job, the present value of his future expected income is V):

$$FW + \gamma V$$

This income continues until the job is terminated. The expected value of a job is then

$$VJ = \frac{FW + \gamma V}{r + \gamma} \qquad (10)$$

This expression follows from the same logic as was used for equation (9). Combining expressions (9) and (10), we have

$$S = rV = \frac{pFW + (r + \gamma)(W_o - C)}{p + r + \gamma} \qquad (11)$$

This expression for search income is identical with that presented in equation (2) except that the full wage in the covered job (FW) is replaced by the money value of the minimum wage (W_m), as the standard model in the text ignored the nonwage aspects of work.

We will now derive the results presented in inequality (8). This inequality expressed the necessary conditions for a minimum wage to raise search income in the standard model when the minimum-wage job is intended to last for only a short time. The value of a job paying W_m per period for n periods will be:

$$VJ = aW_m \qquad (12)$$

where

$$a = \frac{1}{r}\left(1 - \frac{1}{(1 + r)^n}\right)$$

The a term converts each period's income into the present value of the job, where r is the interest rate corresponding to the length of the period. We shall assume that the job searcher looks until he gets a covered job, although the assumption of a shorter planned search

---

X occur with the probability of $1 - p$, given that they have taken place in the previous period. Thus we have the following expected stream of payments:

$$\frac{x}{1 + r} + \frac{(1 - p)}{(1 + r)^2} X + \frac{(1 - p)^2}{(1 + r)^3} X + \dots$$

The sum of this infinite stream is $X/(p + r)$.

period will not affect the results for a marginal labor force participant. Following the logic of expression (9), the present value of search will now be:

$$V = \frac{paW_m + W_o - C}{p + r} \qquad (13)$$

The present value of the expected gain to searching over not working (which is W_o) will be:

$$\text{Expected gain} = \frac{pa(W_m - W_o) - C}{p + r} \qquad (14)$$

For the marginal job searcher, this expected gain equals zero. Letting $S = W_o$ and expression (14) equal zero, the inequality in expression (8) can be derived in the same manner as that in which expression (7) was derived.

It is now possible to derive the reduced-form equation linking the change in the minimum wage to the resulting change in search income for the standard model.

In addition to the assumptions for search income, the standard model assumes that firms do not cut back on their nonwage expenditures. This assumption is standard in most of the minimum-wage models currently in the economic literature. Another common assumption is that uncovered firms lower their full wage whenever they have a surplus of applicants. As a consequence, their workers are assumed to be indifferent to a choice between working and job search. Yet this is clearly unrealistic, since it implies that there are immediate job openings and no unemployment in the uncovered sector—an implication clearly not observable among U.S. youth. In contrast, we will therefore assume that uncovered firms will seek a target "full wage" that causes their average worker to value his job above his value of search. In this way, they can reduce turnover and other costs. As a consequence, unemployment can exist in the uncovered sector in our model presented below.

The reduced-form models will be expressed in elasticity form, since most of the relevant estimates needed to evaluate the parameters of our models are in this form also. We will use the Allen notation;[2] the operator E is a log-derivative operator such that

$$E(x) = d\ln x = dx/x = \text{percent change in } x$$

[2.] R. G. D. Allen, *Mathematical Analysis for Economists* (New York: St. Martin's Press, 1938).

The principal properties of the log-derivative operator are as follows:

$$E(XY) = E(X) + E(Y)$$

and

$$E(X + Y) = \frac{X}{X + Y} E(X) + \frac{Y}{X + Y} E(Y)$$

The following relationships described the main assumptions of the standard model:

a. $L = N_c + U_c + N_u + U_u$

b. $EL = eEV, e > 0$

c. $rV_i = \dfrac{p_i FW_i + (r + \gamma_i)(W_o - C)}{p_i + r + \gamma_i}, i = u, c$

d. $p_i = (\gamma_i + g_i)N_i/U_i, i = u, c$

e. $V_c = V_u = V$

f. $\gamma_i = \bar{\gamma}_i, i = u, c$ (15)

g. $FW_i = W_i (1 - t) + NW_i$

h. $MP_i = W_i + B_i, B_c = \bar{B}_c, i = u, c$

i. $EN_i = \eta_i EMP_i, \eta_i < 0$

j. $FW_u = arV, a = \bar{a}$

k. $W_c = MW$

Relationship (a) is the definition of the labor force as composed of employed workers in the covered sector (N_c) plus the job searchers (or unemployed) in the covered sector (U_c) plus the employed and unemployed in the uncovered sector (N_u, U_u). Relationship (b) states that the changes in labor force participation will be positively related to the changes in the value of search. Relationship (c) follows from expression (11), where FW_i is the full wage in the ith sector.

Relationship (d) describes the factors affecting the probability of getting a job in a given period of search. The available number of jobs is made up of those jobs opened up by workers being separated from their jobs ($\gamma_i N_i$) plus the new jobs being added to the sector

$(g_i N_i$, where g_i is the growth rate in employment). These jobs are assumed to be rationed among the unemployed in their sector. Thus the probability of getting a job in a given period equals the number of job openings $(\gamma_i + g_i)N_i$ divided by the number of unemployed workers (U_i).

Relationship (e) states that job searchers will sort themselves between the covered and uncovered sectors so as to equalize the values of search in both sectors. Relationship (f) states that the separation rates are being held constant.

Relationship (g) defines the full wage as being equal to the worker's after-tax money wage, $W_i (1 - t)$, plus his nonmoney wage, NW_i, which is the value he places on the nonwage aspects of work. Taxes are assumed to be proportional; in the case of progressive tax, the tax rate t would be the marginal tax rate (in expression [g]).

Relationship (h) assumes that firms are competitive such that their marginal products (MP_i) will equal their expenditures on each worker. The expenditures per worker are for money wages (W_i) and for fringe benefits (B_i). (Recall that our definition of fringe benefits is very broad and includes such items as job safety, pleasant working conditions, and on-the-job training.) In the standard model, B_c is assumed to be fixed.

Relationship (i) shows the elasticity of the demand for labor, relating the number of workers to their marginal product. Relationship (j) shows that uncovered employers maintain their workers' full wage at some ratio over their workers' potential income from searching. Note that the assumption that this ratio is fixed $(a = \bar{a})$ corresponds to our assumption that the separation rate in the uncovered sector is also fixed $(\gamma_u = \bar{\gamma}_u)$. Also note that if $a = 1$, $U_u = 0$.

Relationship (k) states that the covered sector's wage is restrained by the minimum wage, MW.

The procedure for the derivation of the reduced-form equation takes three steps. First, the changes in N_c, U_c, N_u, and U_u are solved for in terms of the value of search, V, and the minimum wage, MW. Second, these solutions are combined with the labor force equation. Third, the results of the second step, having only terms in V and MW, are combined to show how V and MW are related.

In the first step, then, we will first solve for the changes in N_c and N_u in terms of V and MW. Using (15) (i), (h), and (k), we have for N_c:

$$EN_c = \eta_c EMP_c = \eta_c \frac{W_c}{W_c + B_c} EW_c = \eta_c \frac{W_c}{W_c + B_c} EMW \qquad (16)$$

Using relationships (15) (i), (h), (j), and (g), we have for N_u:

$$EN_u = \eta_u EMP_u = \eta_u E(W_u + B_u) \tag{17}$$

$$= \eta_u \frac{E(W_u + B_u)}{EFW} EFW = \eta_u EV$$

In this term, it is assumed that uncovered firms are optimally allocating their expenditures between money wages and fringe benefits so that a 10 percent increase in $W_u + B_u$ will increase full wages by 10 percent also. Expression (16) states that the covered firms' employment is affected only by the minimum wage, while expression (15) (h) and (j) states that uncovered firms' employment is affected by their cost per worker, which in turn is determined by the value of search (since the uncovered firms act to change their full wage to maintain a constant ratio between it and the value of search).

Next, in our first step, we wish to solve for U_c and U_u in terms of V and MW. To do this, however, we must first use relationship (15) (c) to get:

$$EV_i = \frac{p_i FW_i}{p_i FW_i + (r + \gamma_i)(W_o - C)} EFW$$

$$+ \left[\frac{p_i FW_i}{p_i FW_i + (r + \gamma_i)(W_o - C)} - \frac{p_i}{p_i + r + \gamma_i} \right] EP_i \tag{18}$$

or

$$EV_i = k_i EFW_i + h_i Ep_i$$

where

$$k_i = \frac{p_i}{p_i + \alpha_i (r + \gamma_i)}$$
$$\alpha_i = (W_o - C)/FW_i, \, \alpha_i \leq 1$$

and

$$h_i = k_i - \frac{p_i}{p_i + r + \gamma_i}, \, h_i > 0$$

This expression breaks the effect of minimum wages into two effects: the full wage effect and the job probability effect. Thus the net effect of minimum wages on the value of search depends upon k_i, which determines the impact of a higher full wage on the value of search, and h_i, which determines the effect of a changed probability of getting a job on the value of search.

The effect of minimum-wage increase on the probability of getting a job is through its effects on employment and unemployment, or, from relationship (15) (c),

$$Ep_i = EN_i - EU_{i}, \qquad i = u, c \qquad (19)$$

Note that expression (19) ignores any transitory effect a minimum increase may have on the basic growth rate in employment.

Combining expressions (16), (18), and (19), we will have:

$$EV_c = k_c EFW + h_c EN_c - h_c EU_c \qquad (20)$$

or

$$EV_c = k_c \frac{W_c}{W_c + B_c} EMW + h_c \, \eta_c \frac{W_c}{W_c + B_c} EMW - h_c \, EU_c$$

or

$$EU_c = \frac{W_c}{W_c + B_c} \left[\frac{k_c}{h_c} + \eta_c \right] EMW - \frac{1}{h_c} EV$$

In the second line, we assume that the cover firm was initially (before the minimum-wage increase) spending an optimal amount on fringe benefits, so that its marginal dollar spent on wages or fringe benefits yielded an increase in the full wage of $1 - t$. Thus, initially,

$$FW_c = (1 - t) (W_c + B_c)$$

or

$$EFW_c = \frac{W_c}{W_c + B_c} EW_c$$

Combining expression (17) with expressions (18) and (19), we will have for U_u:

$$EV_u = k_u EFW_u + h_u EN_u - h_u EU_u \qquad (21)$$

or

$$EV_u = k_u EV + h_u \, \eta_u EV - h_u EU_u$$

or

$$EU_u = \left(\frac{k_u}{h_u} + \eta_u - \frac{1}{h_u} \right) EV$$

92

The second line follows from the fact that $FW_u = (W_u + B_u)(1 - t)$ and that $EV = EFW_u$ for the uncovered firm (from relationship [15]).

In the second step, we first take the log derivative of relationship (15)[3]:

$$EL = \varepsilon EV = \frac{N_c}{L} EN_c + \frac{U_c}{L} EU_c + \frac{N_u}{L} EN_u + \frac{U_u}{L} EU_u \qquad (22)$$

Next the terms derived for EN_c, EU_c, EN_u, and EU_u are substituted in expression (22):

$$
\begin{aligned}
\varepsilon EV = &\frac{N_c}{L} \left[\eta_c \frac{W_c}{W_c + B_c} EMW \right] \\
&+ \frac{U_c}{L} \left[\frac{W_c}{W_c + B_c} \left(\frac{k_c}{h_c} + \eta_c \right) EMW - \frac{1}{h_c} EV \right] \\
&+ \frac{N_u}{L} \left[\eta_u EV \right] \\
&+ \frac{U_u}{L} \left[\left(\frac{k_u}{h_u} + \eta_u - \frac{1}{h_u} \right) EV \right]
\end{aligned}
\qquad (23)
$$

Finally, in the third step, the terms are collected for EV and EMW:

$$
\begin{aligned}
&EV \left(\varepsilon + \frac{U_c}{L} \frac{1}{h_c} - \frac{N_u}{L} \eta_u - \frac{U_u}{L} \frac{k_u}{h_u} - \frac{U_u}{L} \eta_u + \frac{U_u}{L} \frac{1}{h_u} \right) \\
&= EMW \left[\frac{W_c}{W_c + B_c} \left(\frac{L_c}{L} \eta_c + \frac{U_c}{L} \frac{k_c}{h_c} \right) \right]
\end{aligned}
\qquad (24)
$$

where $L_c = N_c + U_c$, the number of labor force participants in the covered sectors.

---

[3] Taking into account the fact that a change in labor force participation will change the nonwork income of the marginal labor force participant (for whom $rV = S = W_o$), which in turn alters change income by:

$$\frac{ES}{EW_o} = \beta$$

where β will be less than unity (as can be easily derived), then the e of relationship b and the ε of this and the following equations will be related by:

$$\varepsilon = \frac{e}{1 - \beta}$$

which will be positive, since e is positive and $\beta < 1$.

The reduced-form equation linking changes in the minimum wage to the value of search is then:

$$\frac{EV}{EMW} = \frac{k_c + h_c \, \eta_c \, \dfrac{1}{u_c}}{\Delta} \tag{25}$$

where

$$\Delta = \frac{L}{L_c} \frac{h_c}{u_c} \frac{W + B_c}{W_c} \left(\varepsilon + \frac{U_c}{L} \frac{1}{h_c} - \frac{U_u}{L} \frac{k_u - 1}{h_u} - \frac{L_u}{L} \eta_u \right) > 0$$

where $L_u = N_u + U_u$ and $u_c = U_c/L_c$, the unemployment rate in the covered sector. Δ is positive since $k_u < 1$ and $\eta < 0$. (Note that in the text, η was given an absolute value, while here we are using its algebraic value.)

As Δ is positive, the sign of the numerator in expression (25) indicates how a minimum-wage increase will affect the welfare of workers. With appropriate substitutions (which will now be described), the sign of the numerator is determined by the inequality used in expression (7). First, for the marginal job searcher, letting $W_o = S$, expression (11) yields the following:

$$1 - \alpha = \frac{p + r + \gamma}{p} \frac{C}{FW}$$

Substituting this expression in the numerator of expression (25) and letting $FW_c = W_m$, $L_c = N_c$ and $-\eta_c = \eta$, we can derive the inequality in expression (7) as a condition for the minimum wage to affect labor force expression positively.

The reduced-form expression for the expanded model is derived as follows.

The expanded model's new assumptions, in addition to those in expression (15), will now be:

$$h' \ MP_i = W_i + B_i$$
$$j' \ FW_u = arV, a = \bar{a}$$
$$FW_c = crV, c = \bar{c}$$

The covered firm is no longer restrained by the assumption that $B_c = B_c$. Instead, like the uncovered firm, it seeks to maintain its full wage at some ratio to the value of search.

Because uncovered firms are not restrained by the minimum wage, they will increase their fringe benefits until an additional dollar of expenditures on fringe benefits will increase the worker's full wage by the same amount as an additional dollar of money wages. Thus

$$FW_u = (1 - t)(W_u + B_u)$$

The covered firm will be restrained by the minimum wage from reducing its wages, however, and will thus supply fewer fringe benefits. As a consequence, its marginal fringe benefit will yield a larger increase in utility to the worker.

$$dFW_c = dNW_c > (1 - t)dB_c \qquad (26)$$

or

$$\frac{dNW_c}{dB_c} = \frac{dFW_c}{dB} = b(1 - t) \text{ where } b \geqq 1 \text{ when } B_c < B_c^*$$

where B_c^* is the optimal level of fringe benefits (corresponding to Q_c in figure 1). Thus for the covered sector:

$$FW_c = (1 - t)(W_c + bNW_c) \qquad (27)$$

Note that if fringe benefits are perfect substitutes for money wages, b will equal 1.

The derivation of the expanded model's reduced-form equation follows the same three steps as the standard model's derivation did.

One of the main differences is that, in the first step, we now have for N_c:

$$EN_c = \eta_c EMP_c = \eta_c E(W_c + B_c) \qquad (28)$$

$$= \frac{b - 1}{b} \eta_c \frac{W_c}{W_c + B_c} EMW + \frac{1}{b} \eta_c \frac{W_c + bB_c}{W_c + B_c} EV$$

The second line of expression (28) is derived from expression (27):

$$dFW_c = (1 - t)dW_c + b(1 - t)dB_c$$

or

$$crdV = (1 - t)dMW + b(1 - t)dB_c$$

so that

$$dB_c = \frac{cr}{b(1 - t)} dV - \frac{1}{b} dMW$$

Therefore,

$$dW_c + dB_c = dMW + \frac{cr}{b(1 - t)} - \frac{1}{b} dMW$$

or

$$\frac{d(W_c + B_c)}{W_c + B_c} = \frac{MW}{W_c + B_c} \frac{b - 1}{b} EMW + \frac{rcV}{b(1 - t)} \frac{1}{W_c + b_c} EV$$

or

$$E(W_c + B_c) = \frac{W_c}{W_c + B_c} \frac{b - 1}{b} EMW + \frac{W_c + bB_c}{b(W_c + B_c)} EV$$

This expression was used in expression (28). The other main difference between the derivations of the standard and the expanded models is the expression for U_c:

$$EV_c = k_c EFW_c + h_c EN_c - hEU_c \qquad (29)$$

or

$$EV = k_c EV + h_c \left[\frac{b - 1}{b} \eta_c \frac{W_c}{W_c + B_c} EMW + \frac{1}{b} \eta_c \frac{W_c + bB_c}{W_c + B_c} EV \right]$$
$$- h_c EU_c$$

or

$$EU_c = \left(\frac{k_c - 1}{h_c} + \frac{1}{b} \eta_c \frac{W_c + bB_c}{W_c + B_c} \right) EV + \frac{b - 1}{b} \eta_c \frac{W_c}{W_c + B_c} EMW$$

The second step combines the labor force expression with our expressions for N_c and U_c (derived above) and N_u and U_u (derived in the previous section):

$$EL = \varepsilon EV$$
$$= \frac{U_c}{L} \left[\left(\frac{k_c - 1}{h_c} + \frac{1}{b} \eta_c \frac{W_c + bB_c}{W_c + B_c} \right) EV \right.$$
$$\left. + \frac{b - 1}{b} \eta_c \frac{W_c}{W_c + B_c} EMW \right]$$
$$+ \frac{N_c}{L} \left[\frac{b - 1}{b} \eta_c \frac{W_c}{W_c + B_c} EMW + \frac{1}{b} \frac{W_c + bB_c}{W_c + B_c} EV \right] \qquad (30)$$
$$+ \frac{U_u}{L} \left[\left(\frac{k_u - 1}{h_u} + \eta_u \right) EV \right]$$
$$+ \frac{N_u}{L} \left[\eta_u EV \right]$$

In the third step, the MW and V terms are collected:

$$EV\left(\varepsilon - \frac{U_c}{L}\frac{k_c - 1}{h_c} - \frac{L_c}{L}\frac{1}{b}\eta_c\frac{W_c + bB_c}{W_c + B_c} - \frac{U_u}{L}\frac{k_u - 1}{h_u} - \frac{L_u}{L}\eta_u\right)$$

$$= EMW\left(\frac{L_c}{L}\frac{W_c}{W_c + B_c}\eta_c\frac{b - 1}{b}\right) \qquad (31)$$

The reduced-form equation for the expanded model is thus:

$$\frac{EV}{EMW} = \frac{\eta_c\dfrac{b - 1}{b}}{\Delta_2} \qquad (32)$$

where

$$\Delta_2 = \frac{L}{L_c}\frac{W_c + B_c}{W_c}\left(\varepsilon - \frac{U_c}{L}\frac{k_c - 1}{h_c} - \frac{L_c}{L}\frac{1}{b}\eta_c\frac{W_c + bB_c}{W_c + B_c}\right.$$

$$\left. - \frac{U_u}{L}\frac{k_u - 1}{h_u} - \frac{L_u}{L}\eta_u\right)$$

where $\Delta_2 > 0$ as $k_c < 1$ and $\eta_i < 0$.

The sign of expression (32) is negative, since η_c is negative and b is greater than one. It follows that in the expanded model a minimum-wage increase will always reduce search income and hence full wages in all jobs.

A NOTE ON THE BOOK

The typeface used for the text of this book is
Palatino, designed by Hermann Zapf.
The type was set by
FotoTypesetters, Incorporated, of Baltimore.
Thomson-Shore, Inc., of Dexter, Michigan, printed
and bound the book, using Warren's Olde Style paper.
The cover and format were designed by Pat Taylor.
The manuscript was edited by Marcia Brubeck, and
by Claire Theune of the AEI Publications staff.

SELECTED AEI PUBLICATIONS

AEI ASSOCIATES PROGRAM

The American Enterprise Institute invites your participation in the competition of ideas through its AEI Associates Program. This program has two objectives:

The first is to broaden the distribution of AEI studies, conferences, forums, and reviews, and thereby to extend public familiarity with the issues. AEI Associates receive regular information on AEI research and programs, and they can order publications and cassettes at a savings.

The second objective is to increase the research activity of the American Enterprise Institute and the dissemination of its published materials to policy makers, the academic community, journalists, and others who help shape public attitudes. Your contribution, which in most cases is partly tax deductible, will help ensure that decision makers have the benefit of scholarly research on the practical options to be considered before programs are formulated. The issues studied by AEI include:

- Defense Policy
- Economic Policy
- Energy Policy
- Foreign Policy
- Government Regulation
- Health Policy
- Legal Policy
- Political and Social Processes
- Social Security and Retirement Policy
- Tax Policy

For more information, write to:

AMERICAN ENTERPRISE INSTITUTE
1150 Seventeenth Street, N.W.
Washington, D.C. 20036